The Four-Blocks®
Literacy Model

Writing Mini-Lessons for Upper Grades:
The Big-Blocks™ Approach
by
Dorothy P. Hall, Patricia M. Cunningham,
and
Amanda B. Arens

Carson-Dellosa Publishing Company, Inc.
Greensboro, North Carolina

Credits

Editor:
Joey Bland

Layout Design:
Joey Bland

Artist:
Wayne Miller

Cover Design:
Ray Lambert

ISBN 0-88724-124-7

Dedication

To my husband, Jeff:

Each day with you is a blessing. You are my life and my joy, and I am so happy to share it all with you. Thank you for your encouragement, your patience, and your support in my endeavor. Without you, I just couldn't do it. I love you . . . beyond words.

Amanda Arens

This book is also dedicated to all of the upper-grades teachers, who take the time to model writing **for** their students. We know that by showing your students how you think as you write, both on self-selected topics and for focused writing, you are helping your students become better writers. The goal of this book is to capture these lessons, so that all teachers gain this skill and more students profit from writing mini-lessons in the upper grades.

Dottie Hall, Amanda Arens, and Pat Cunningham

Table of Contents

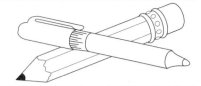

Table of Contents

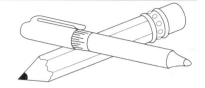

Introduction

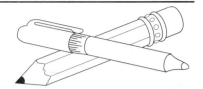

By the time students are in the upper grades they are expected to be able to both read and write on grade level. Many students can do this; others cannot. Content area reading and writing almost always demand that students read grade-level text and write grade-level responses. Textbooks in the content areas are usually written on or above grade level. Thus, some students find themselves falling further and further behind in school. Writing is one area of the curriculum that can be a multi-level activity if teachers allow students to choose their topics, accept what students can do, and help them to become better writers. In the upper grades, students often need to respond to reading by writing, so choice is not always an option. When teachers can, however, they should give students the choice of what to write about. When students write on topics of their own choosing, they grow as writers, and teachers can observe that growth by looking at writing samples over time.

If you have students who have had opportunities to write daily since kindergarten, you may have students that like to write and can write quite well. If you have students who have not had many opportunities to write or who have only written to story starters or prompts, you may have students who do not like to write. Teachers in the upper grades usually have students on a variety of writing levels and with a variety of attitudes toward writing. Writer's Workshop (Calkins, 1994) is one approach to writing that all students seem to like! In Writer's Workshop, the students learn to "tell about" the many things they know or are learning about. They tell about ideas, friends, dreams, favorites, secrets, fears, etc. They learn to write stories, poems, letters, biographies, informational pieces, and more. They learn to write, and sometimes they take a piece through the writing process and learn how to "make it better" by revising, editing, and publishing that piece. Grammar, mechanics, organization, voice, and different genres can be taught in the context of real writing, and the students actually understand what we are teaching them! Some students actually get excited about writing and appreciate knowing the mechanics and techniques that will help them become better writers.

When a writing program works and students are excited about writing, we usually see teachers who write for their students and share their writing with their students. They personally experience all of the steps in the writing process with their students from finding a topic to publishing the finished piece. The teachers also carefully construct the writing environment so that students know what to expect and what is expected of them. Then, the teacher expects that all students will write and take responsibility for their own writing but is there to offer help when it is needed. Teachers talk to their students about writing in conversation, just as they would like students to talk to each other. In conferences, they listen to the writer and the writing and ask the kind of questions that will enable writers to think about what they have done and what they want to do next. They put editorial concerns in the proper place, after the content is written and revised. In the upper grades, the first editor of any piece should be the writer. Then, the teacher edits during a conference, so that the writer and the teacher can have a conversation about the writing.

There is so much to teach in the upper grades—including new content and reviewing what the students have learned in previous years—the teacher must integrate to get it all done. The teacher must also look at the students she is teaching and find out just what they know, what must be reviewed, and what needs to be taught.

What is a Mini-Lesson?

Lucy Calkins (1986) came up with the idea of mini-lessons. The term "mini" means brief. Writer's Workshop always begins with a mini-lesson. This mini-lesson is a brief meeting where the teacher addresses an issue with the whole class. That issue may have arisen from a previous lesson or from looking at students' writing in progress. In the mini-lesson the teacher usually models and shares how he thinks and writes. It is also a time when the teacher talks about issues of process or technique, like the difference between revising and recopying.

The lessons in this book are designed to last approximately 10 minutes, just long enough to touch on a timely topic. Each lesson focuses on an issue or skill that students need to know or be reminded of if they are to become better writers. This is a time for the teacher to do the work and the students to watch. After the mini-lesson, the students will have their chance to write. The teacher will coach them or become their editor by showing them things that they could improve and helping them see what they should do and why. On some days in the upper grades, students will write on self-selected topics. On other days, students will focus on writing something under the teacher's direction. After each mini-lesson, the student is asked to write and grow as a writer. The purpose of this book is to help teachers with the variety of mini-lessons available to upper-grades teachers. There are three kinds of mini-lessons in this book: procedures, conventions, and craft.

Procedures mini-lessons help students know what they need to do during Writer's Workshop to become better writers. At the beginning of the school year, procedures mini-lessons usually include how to use the daily writing folder or notebook, coming up with a writer's list, what resources and materials are available to the writer, how to revise and edit, etc.

Mini-lessons on conventions are also needed. Conventions are mechanics, such as punctuation, capitalization, and spelling. The lessons a teacher has to do depend on the experience that the class, as a whole, has with writing. Capitalizing titles may be needed by one fourth-grade class but not by another fourth-grade class. During mini-lessons, we teach skills but only those that are needed and only when we see a need for it in our students' writing. Conventions lessons may include mini-lessons on punctuation, usage, and spelling. Look at your students' writing to decide if they need a lesson on how to write paragraph or how to use capital letters. Another place to find what to teach is your curriculum. If your state or school system has a list of conventions to be taught or mastered at each grade level, teach them during your mini-lessons. For some topics, you will need to do more than one lesson. You will need to reteach those conventions that your students don't know or use daily.

Craft mini-lessons touch on matters of technique, style, and genre. Different kinds of writing call for different criteria as students learn more about what makes short stories, poetry, fiction, and nonfiction. Mini-lessons are a time when the different concepts of modes and genres are introduced, usually after reading selections aloud during a teacher read-aloud. In Big-Blocks™ classrooms, this would happen during Self-Selected Reading. Then, the teacher would model this type of writing during the mini-lesson. Showing students the different techniques writers use helps the students develop a repertoire of their own strategies and techniques. After applying these strategies several times in their own writing, we hope that the strategies will become second nature.

Focused Writing Mini-Lessons

When doing focused writing lessons in the upper grades, the teacher does several lessons on the chosen topic or genre. The teacher spends several days showing the students all of the steps a writer takes to write this genre. There are many different kinds of writing, so we don't cover all of them in this book. We do show you how we would take students through a process rather than just giving them an assignment and expecting all students to know how to write and what to do when writing a particular genre. At the end of each lesson, we suggest several ways to use this genre at different grade levels.

How to Use this Book

Writing Mini-Lessons for Upper Grades was written to be useful to teachers with a wide range of writers in their classes. Because we have not seen your students nor had an opportunity to examine their writing, we cannot tell you exactly which mini-lessons they will need or how many mini-lessons they will need on a particular strategy or technique. We have designed the book to provide a variety of mini-lessons your students might need. Trust your judgment to pick and choose how many mini-lessons and which ones. The mini-lessons are divided into three sections: Early in the Year—Getting Started, Most of the Year—Continuing to Write, and Later in the Year—Getting Better.

Early in the Year—Getting Started

The mini-lessons for early in the year are designed to teach basic procedures and review mechanical and grammatical conventions that your students should already know and can get up to speed on after a quick review and reminder. If, after teaching these early mini-lessons, you discover by observing your students' writing, that they have not learned these basic mechanical and grammatical conventions, you will need to spend more time teaching them. Additional suggestions are included for each topic. As you teach these early-in-the year mini-lessons, students will be writing on self-selected topics. The techniques and strategies taught will apply to all types of writing, and students should be expected to apply them in their writing. During these early lessons, the Writer's Checklist will be started with items that most students have mastered. Items should be added gradually to the checklist, and each student should do a quick edit each day for the items on the checklist.

Most of the Year—Continuing to Write

The mini-lessons for most of the year assume that students will be spending some time in self-selected writing on topics of their own choosing and some time on focused writing on topics and genres chosen by the teacher. Lessons are included to teach students how to write a memoir, a letter, poetry, book and movie reviews, a biography, an informational article, and a "how-to" piece. Lessons are also included on writing to a prompt. These lessons can be adapted to help you prepare for whatever kinds of writing tasks are required by your curriculum or your mandated writing assessments. If you think your class needs one of these sets of lessons earlier in the year, you can move that set up depending on the class and grade level.

Later in the Year—Getting Better

Mini-lessons for later in the year are the "icing on the cake." Students learn how their writing can be a gift to someone they care about, how journals and diaries can help them sharpen their writing and reflect on their experiences, and how to write traditional tales. The year ends with a publishing and author celebration in which students savor their accomplishments and reflect on how far they have come as writers.

Early in the Year–Getting Started

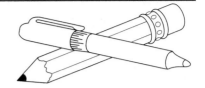

Mini-Lessons for Early in the Year

The mini-lessons for early in the year are designed to teach basic procedures and review mechanical and grammatical conventions that your students should already know and can get up to speed on after a quick review and reminder. If, after teaching these early mini-lessons, you discover by observing your students' writing, that they have not learned these basic mechanical and grammatical conventions, you will need to spend more time teaching them. Additional suggestions are included for each topic. As you teach these early-in-the year mini-lessons, students will be writing on self-selected topics. The techniques and strategies taught will apply to all types of writing, and students should be expected to apply them in their writing. During these early lessons, the Writer's Checklist will be started with items that most students have mastered. Items should be added gradually to the checklist, and each student should do a quick edit each day for the items on the checklist.

Mini-Lessons in this Section

Modeling How to Write Using a Think-Aloud

Creating a List of Topics

Prewriting Using a Think-Aloud

Using a Think-Aloud to Write after Mapping

Procedures for Writer's Workshop

Creating a Writing Handbook

Author's Chair

Using a Think-Aloud for Beginning Capitalization and Ending Punctuation

What to Do about Spelling

Editing Your Writing with a Writer's Checklist

Making Decisions about What to Write

Different Writing Genres

Sentences that Make Sense and Stay on Topic

Writing Process

Self-Editing and Peer Editing

Capital Letters for Titles, Specific People, Events, and Places

Mini-Lesson Focus: Modeling How to Write Using a Think-Aloud (Craft/Conventions)

On the first day of school many upper-grades teachers wonder, "How well do the students in my class write?" To find out, teachers often get a writing sample. Some teachers assign their students a topic such as, "Write about your summer vacation" or "Write about yourself." When given a topic, some students begin the assigned task quickly, other students will think to themselves, "I didn't go anywhere!" or "I don't know what to write about me." Students, at all grade levels, need to understand that writing is putting down on paper what you want to tell. Think-alouds are a great way to further upper-grades students' understanding that writing is just telling about things. They also show students how to think and what to think about when writing.

The teacher says:

"I am your new teacher and you don't know a lot about me, but you will soon know more. Today, I am going to write for you and tell you about me."

The teacher thinks aloud and writes:

"I indent my first paragraph and begin my sentence with a capital letter." (She does each thing as she says it.) My name is Mrs. Amanda Arens. "I put a capital letter at the beginning of **Mrs.**, **Amanda**, and **Arens** because names always begin with capitals and so do titles. I end my sentence with a period because telling sentences always end that way.

"My next sentence starts with a capital and so does my husband's first and last names. I put another period at the end of that sentence. The word **husband's** needs an apostrophe before the s to show possession." (She talks as she writes.) My husband's name is Jeff Arens. "My next sentence starts with a capital and ends with a period." He has his own business and loves to work on the computer. "Some words are easy to spell like **he**, **has**, **his**, **to**, **on**, and **the**. Other words I have to think of the spelling or stretch out and think of the letters that represent those sounds, like **own**, **business**, and **com-pu-ter**." (She continues telling the class about her family, their names, and something about them. She remembers to talk about capitalization, punctuation, and spelling.) I have three children. My daughter is the oldest. Merrill Kaye is your age and loves to read. I have two sons who are younger. Their names are Alex and Lafe.

"I indent my second paragraph and begin my sentence with a capital letter." (She does each thing as she says it and tells them about where she lives and what it is like and continues to write and talk.) I live outside of town in a brick house. We have a small lake in our back yard. We have lots of land and not many neighbors. We like living away from town. But that means my husband and I do lots of driving. We have to drive to church, to work, to stores, and to ball games. Whenever we do anything, we have to drive there.

As she writes, the teacher thinks aloud about the process she is using. She models and talks about using capitals and periods. The teacher also uses this opportunity to stop and think about how words are spelled and to str-e-tch out a word or two to show the students how you can do this when you don't know how to spell a word. Because she thinks aloud as she writes, more and more students will understand and use the processes she models and talks about. After her mini-lessons, the teacher invites the students to write for her. Many tell about themselves, but some may write on other topics.

Other Ideas for Modeling How to Write Using a Think-Aloud

Using Literature for Modeling Think-Alouds

Read *How I Spent My Summer Vacation* by Mark Teague (Crowne Publishing, 1996) during a teacher read-aloud. At writing time, begin your mini-lesson by saying, "This morning I read *How I Spent My Summer Vacation* and you wanted to talk about your summer vacations. So, I thought to myself, When it is writing time, I am going to tell the class about my family's vacation to the lake region in Upper Michigan. The story I read was a made-up story, but my story is true. Here is how I spent my summer vacation."

> In June, as soon as school was out in Missouri, my family went to Michigan. We drove all the way to the upper part of Lake Michigan. It was . . . .

Beginning Capitals and Periods at the Ends of Sentences

In some mini-lessons, you will want to focus on one particular part of the writing process. For example, you can think aloud focusing on beginning capitals and periods. Write something and think aloud about the use of capital letters and periods. Many students have not written all summer and need this reminder.

"Today, I am going to write about fourth (or fifth) grade. I will begin my first sentence with a capital **F**." Fourth (or fifth) grade is the best grade. "I end my sentence with a period and begin my next sentence with a capital **I**." In fourth (or fifth) grade we learn all about our state (or our country, our geographic neighbors, etc.).

Capital Letters for Names (People, Books, Movies, etc.) and I

Talk and write about people you know or characters in a book or movie, and only think aloud about how you capitalize names and I. Toward the end of the lesson, stop and ask the students what kind of letter you should use to begin names and I.

> This weekend I went to see the new Harry Potter movie with my family. It is a movie based on the second Harry Potter book titled, <u>Harry Potter and the Chamber of Secrets</u>. It has the same characters as in the first book and movie: Harry Potter, Ron, the Weasleys, and Hermione.

When you get to the name of the movie or book, the names of characters, or the word I, ask the students what you should do. Let them "help" you by telling you that names and the word I need beginning capital letters. You can even share the pen and ask a student to come up and write that word or name.

A Period Is Used after Abbreviations

Some students in the upper grades need to be reminded about this. Write one day and focus on thinking aloud about abbreviations and putting a period after them.

> Mr. and Mrs. Logan were heading for Dr. Ray's office on Reynolda Rd. They took a wrong turn and ended up on Miller Dr. Now they were lost.

Mini-Lesson Focus: Creating a List of Topics (Procedures)

People write best when they write about the things they know about. When teachers assign topics, they create a welfare system, putting students on writers' welfare (Graves, 1983). A teacher can work on ways to avoid hearing, "I don't know what to write about." This mini-lesson models the process for making decisions on writing ideas and invites students to begin their own lists. The teacher will either bring in a list of her own writing ideas or will create a list in front of the students. It is important to make the items on the list narrow in focus. Young students often write about things in general: family, school, ball games, places, etc. As students get older, it is important that their writing is more specific. Talk through your decisions, sharing bits of information as to why the event or topic is on the list. Give thought to the list ahead of time, if the list won't already be prepared before class. Once started, it is a list that you will want a permanent copy of, so you can add and refer to it throughout the year.

The teacher says:

"Today, I want to share with you my list of writing ideas. There are lots of things I would like to write about; in fact, some I already have, and some are works in progress. But, today what I really want to show you is **how** I decide what to put on my list.

"I have found out that I write better when I am writing about things that really matter to me or things I've actually done. But, I've done a lot of things in my life, and I have a lot of experiences to choose from. So, when I decide to write about one of those things, it usually is a very strong memory for me. For example, the first thing on my list is my husband, Jeff. I didn't just put his name on my list. I've been married to Jeff for 13 years, and I've known him for 17 years, so I have so many memories with him. However, I've chosen a couple that stand out in my mind. Even though it was 17 years ago, I clearly remember the night we met. I hope to write about it someday because it may not be clear for much longer. Another idea I have for writing is to tell how Jeff makes our children sing a song to him when he is playing with them. If he traps them, the 'magic word' is to sing 'Daddy is a handsome man' to the tune of 'Camptown Races.'

"Or, I could tell the story of the day this summer when Alex was collecting leaves for a project at art camp, picked poison ivy, brought it home, and his sister and dad helped him press it in some books. Oh, they were all so miserable for the next few days.

"I've already written a poem about my mother's laughing brown eyes. And, I journaled in a scrapbook about Jeff and the changes I've seen in him. That is why you see both of those items checked off.

My Writing Ideas	
Jeff	the night we met at Singsations tryouts
	hearing him sing "The Lord's Prayer"
	"Daddy is a handsome man, doo-dah"
	✔ The changes in him since we moved
Merrill Kaye	her love of books
	the talking trash can at Disney World
	being chased by wild geese
Alex	the perfectionist
	becoming an artist, its ups and downs
	collecting the poison ivy
Lafe	swimming in the "cat pool"
	"It's just what boys do!"
	my little sugar bear
Mother	how I miss her
	✔ her laughing brown eyes
	her ability to express herself
Ma-ma	the last jar of raspberry jelly
	a list of my favorite foods
	no time to mourn
Teaching	watching the "light bulb come on"
	adults are my new students
Professional life	working on a book of mini-lessons for upper grades

Writing Mini-Lessons for Upper Grades: The Big-Blocks™ Approach

"This is a list I keep going back to. I add ideas. I write about some and check them off. Now, it is time to send you all to write today. If you would like to make your list of ideas, that is a great way to go. If you already have a specific idea, you may begin working on it, or if you're in the middle of something, you may continue working on it."

The teacher sends the students to their desks to write. Many students will begin to create their own lists of writing ideas. Some won't be as specific as suggested. Some will list things such as "my family vacation," "my pet," etc. Soon, the teacher will be doing another mini-lesson on making the focus sharper. Eventually, the teacher will want all of her students to have a list of writing ideas that they will keep with their writing. She wants them to go back to this list on the days when they want to say, "I don't know what to write about!"

Other Ideas for What to Write About

Sharing Another Student's List(s)

Be sure to circulate as the students write their lists during the previous mini-lesson. Watch for students who find making a list an easy task. Conference with one or two of these students, and find out if they are willing to share their lists. Sharing one student's list may help other students think that they have had some of the same experiences or know about similar topics. This sharing mini-lesson can help other students add more to their writing lists.

I'm an Expert

Students in the upper grades can often tell you some things they are good at doing: playing basketball or soccer, singing, playing computer games, writing, etc. They also might know a lot about several topics: the *Titanic*, dinosaurs (a certain kind?), snakes (Do they know more about specific kinds of snakes?), baseball (Do they know a lot about certain teams or players?), etc. The things they know a lot about, the things they are interested in, and things they can do quite well can form the basis for "I'm an expert on . . . ." lists. Next to each big topic they need to write some specific things they might write about. Let your students know what you know a lot about and what you are an expert on (making pumpkin bread, snickerdoodle cookies, or pecan tarts; crocheting afghans; wallpapering; etc.). Write something about what you do quite well and model for your students how you write about it.

Keeping a Class List of Interesting Topics on a Chart or in a Jar

Every time your class learns something new in social studies, science, math, health, or current events, that "something" can be added to the class list on a chart or written on a piece of paper and added to a "topic jar." Occasionally choose a topic for your mini-lesson from the class writing list or from the "topic jar."

Using Memories

Read Jamie Lee Curtis's book, *When I Was Little: A Four-Year-Old's Memory of Her Youth* (HarperCollins, 1993). Then, write about one of your memories, real or not—no one will know! Invite the students to add stories from their young lives to their lists and choose one to write about. (Have them talk to their parents if they cannot remember any stories; everyone has a story to tell!)

Remember: students have a daily choice to either write more about a topic (add on to a piece) or start a new piece.

Mini-Lesson Focus: Prewriting Using a Think-Aloud (Craft)

It is important to model for students the process of writing. One effective mode of modeling is to use a think-aloud. The think-aloud allows students to see and hear what is happening as you make decisions as you write. Think-alouds become easier with practice, as does writing. Choose a topic from your writing list to begin the process of writing with your students. Explain why you choose that particular topic (for example, it is important to you, you have very vivid memories of it, etc.). Then, model the steps of the writing process—what you are doing and why—that you want your students to see or be aware of as they write.

The teacher says:

"Today, I want to write about something from my writing list. I was looking over my ideas last night and decided I really want to write about the day Merrill Kaye was chased by the Canada geese. I think it would be helpful if I have some method of organizing my thoughts about the events. When we prewrite or brainstorm, sometimes it is helpful to choose a way to organize those thoughts. I have a simple story map that sometimes helps me make sure I have included several important elements of a story." (Begins to fill in the map and talks through it.)

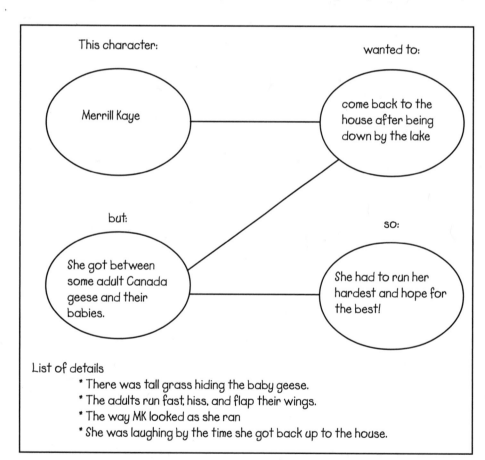

This character:

Merrill Kaye

wanted to:

come back to the house after being down by the lake

but:

She got between some adult Canada geese and their babies.

so:

She had to run her hardest and hope for the best!

List of details
* There was tall grass hiding the baby geese.
* The adults run fast, hiss, and flap their wings.
* The way MK looked as she ran
* She was laughing by the time she got back up to the house.

"After I map the story out this way, it helps me remember things I want to include. I know there are other details I will include to make the story more interesting, but I also know stories need a problem and solution to be more interesting.

"Let me add a few of those details to my map so I won't forget them; then tomorrow I will begin to write my story. I'll just make a list, and as I write, I'll decide where they fit in best.

"I really think it helps my writing if I do this kind of thinking before I start. It helps me get an idea of where to go with my story and what kinds of things I want to include.

"Tomorrow, I'll begin writing this story (page 16). If some of you are ready to start a new story or have had some trouble going on with your story, you might try "mapping" out your ideas during writing time today."

Students go off to write, and some will choose to use the organizer the teacher has modeled. From time to time, she might even require that students use organizers of some kind to help in the development of an idea.

Other Ideas for Prewriting

Using a Web

Webs are often used to organize information. Some students may have had instruction in using a web; others may not. If your class is studying a state or province, the United States, Canada, Mexico, or Central America, you want students to write reports at some point in the year. A web can help organize all of the information they gather. One way to help all students is to model this process. First, put the topic in the center. Then, decide what areas must be included in this report; those areas become the "spokes" of your web. What you need to include about these topics is written around these spokes. Students will understand how to do this and follow your lead if you model this for them and begin a web using **your** curriculum.

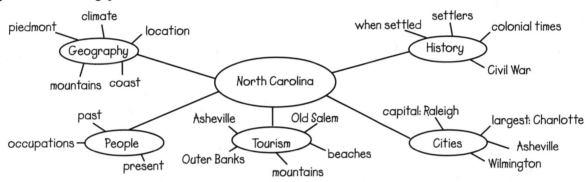

Using a Venn Diagram to Tell about Similarities and Differences

A Venn diagram can be used to compare two things. You can use it to compare two books or two authors you have read during Guided Reading. You can use a Venn diagram to compare two cities in your state or province, two regions of a country, or maybe two different leaders or wars in history. Use a Venn diagram to organize the information, then write about those two stories, authors, people, places, times, etc.

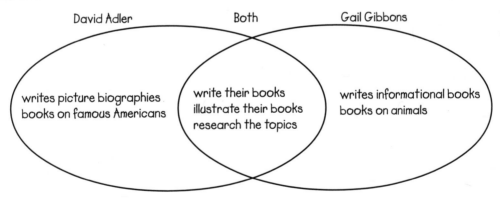

Using a Comparison Chart to Compare Two or More People, Places, Things, or Times

The teacher and the class can fill out the comparison chart together and use this chart to organize the information and write the paragraphs in a paper or pages in a report.

Place	Location	Climate	Size	Population	Occupations	Tourism
Canada						
United States						
Mexico						

Mini-Lesson Focus: Using a Think-Aloud to Write after Mapping a Story (Craft)

Use a graphic organizer you've created (page 14) and begin writing the story. You should refer to the organizer frequently, even checking off things you've included. You need to talk about what you are writing and how you are deciding what to write. Model rereading your text to see if it makes sense, making marks to make changes, etc.

The teacher says:

"I'm ready to write my story about Merrill Kaye, today. I noticed I was thinking about it even last night at home. I think it was on my mind because I spent the time yesterday making my map.

"I never write my title first; I always wait until later or even until I'm done with the story. I think my titles are better if I wait.

"I think I need to tell the reader that Merrill Kaye has been watching the geese take care of their babies for about a month.

"I see that I've already included details I didn't put on my list. Sometimes, those details don't come to me until I start writing."

Title?

Merrill Kaye trudged along the dam at the edge of the lake. Dusk was approaching, and she was ready to head back to the house. Not far from the edge of the bank, close to the tall grass, she saw Momma Goose and Daddy Goose.

For the past month, Merrill Kaye had been watching the geese take care of their babies. She knew they were pretty protective, and the babies always obeyed their parents.

"That is all I have time to write today. Some of you may have an idea for a story that you have mapped out. Hopefully, you can see how that will guide your writing. It is okay to include more details than you've written on your lists. Just refer back to the lists and the maps to keep you going."

Other Ideas for Using a Think-Aloud to Write after Prewriting

Using a Think-Aloud to Write after Creating a Venn Diagram

After making a Venn diagram with the class about two authors (page 15). You can use it to begin to write.

David Adler and Gail Gibbons write informational books for children. David writes mainly picture biographies. He has written about many of the people we learn about in American history: George Washington, Benjamin Franklin, Thomas Jefferson, and Abraham Lincoln. He . . . .

Gail Gibbons writes informational books about things children are interested in. Cats, Dogs, Polar Bears, Penguins, and Spiders are some of her popular books. She . . . .

Both writers spend time researching their topics. Then, they write and illustrate their books.

You may want to take three days to write this, a day on each author and his or her work and then a final day on how they are alike.

Using a Think-Aloud to Write after Creating a Comparison Chart

If you created a comparison chart in social studies to compare several regions of the United States or the provinces in Canada, then you could use the chart to begin to write a paragraph (or page) about each region or province and territory.

Canada

Canada has many provinces and territories: British Columbia, Yukon, Northwest Territories, Alberta, Saskatchewan, Manitoba, Ontario, Nunavut, Quebec, New Brunswick, Newfoundland and Labrador, Nova Scotia, and Prince Edward Island.

Using a Think-Aloud to Reread and Revise

Each day that you return to the same piece of writing, you can model and think aloud about the importance of rereading what has been written so far. If you find things that don't make sense, make changes. You may eliminate some sentences because you decide they don't fit the topic or aren't as important as you first thought. This type of revision may seem less cumbersome than the revision often done at the **end** of writing. Taking on the revision in small chunks seems easier, and many students find this works well for them.

Using a Think-Aloud to Model Correct Punctuation

Write for the class and talk about the punctuation. What ending punctuation are you using and why? Are you using commas? Why? Are you writing about a conversation? Why? Are you using quotation marks for the dialogue? Why? Share with them how you think as you write and how you remember to use quotation marks each time a person talks.

Using a Think-Aloud to Model What to Do about Spelling

Students at every grade level need to be reminded about spelling. Writers spell the best they can when drafting—except for word wall words or words in their personal dictionaries, if they have them. The real dictionary is used during editing, not while writing the first draft!

Mini-Lesson Focus: Procedures for Writer's Workshop (Procedures)

Beginning the year with procedures in place will help your Writing Block run smoothly. Procedures will need to be determined by the teacher and then modeled for the class. In the following lessons, certain procedures are modeled because of their importance in supporting your students and in helping you organize the Writing time. Do some thinking about how and where you will want students to keep their writing. Will it be collected and distributed each day? Providing a predictable structure supports all students when writing each day. Some say this is their longest mini-lesson of the year!

Folders or Notebooks

Some teachers prefer to have students write on paper and keep those papers in a folder. Students often need two folders, one a "permanent" folder and one a "works-in-progress" folder. In the upper grades, two folders works quite well as students go back and forth between self-selected topics and focused pieces. Sometimes the two folders represent the two types of writing that the students are asked to do and are labeled: Self-Selected Topics and Focused Writing. When a teacher chooses a notebook (bound or loose-leaf), it often has to be divided into two sections so a student does not have to hunt through the notebook to find self-selected topics after completing a focused piece. Whatever the teacher chooses, she must explain how she will use the folders or notebooks and why.

Name and Date on Papers

Each time you write during a mini-lesson, be sure to use the procedure you have developed for your students. Because you will be collecting writing throughout the year, the date helps keep the writing in order. Dating daily work is critically important. For a piece that is worked on for multiple days, you may want a procedure for dating that piece each time it is worked on. This helps you see how much time is devoted to each piece. As always, names are important, just in case a piece of writing slips out of the writing folder and lands on the floor! There is no right or wrong way or place to have the name and date recorded; just decide and keep it consistent.

The teacher says:

"Each day as you begin to write, it will be very important that you make sure your name and the date are on your papers. Just as I am having you do in all other subject areas, I want your name to appear on the upper right-hand corner

> Mrs. Arens
> 8/29/02

of your paper. The date will be written right under your name, using numbers. Look at the overhead where I have begun writing. I have modeled writing my name and date, just the way I expect you to write yours.

"If you come back to this piece of writing more than once, you'll need to date it each time. I would like for those dates to be in the left-hand margin, written in numbers again. It will help you know what you worked on each day, and I'll know how many days you spent with each piece of writing. At the end of the year, you'll enjoy looking back at your work, and having a date on each piece will help us keep it in order."

Writing on Every Other Line

Consider this a non-negotiable item! Everyone writes on every other line, no questions asked. This rule is for drafting only. If you have ever tried to help a student edit or revise on a paper with every bit of available space filled, you know the stress it can cause. So, insist that your students write on every other line. They will need daily reminders for a good part of the year. Just like all other procedures, introduce this in a mini-lesson.

The teacher says:

"When you are writing this year, it will be very important for you to write on every other line on your paper. Sometimes you will forget, and it won't be necessary to erase what you've written. But, as **soon** as you remember, begin writing on every other line. It is so much easier to go back to what you've written and make changes if you leave space.

"One way I remind myself is to take my pencil and just put a dot on every other line. Then, I can write on the lines without dots. It is fine with me if any of you would like to remind yourself that way. It is a procedure I will ask you to use all year long."

Using Cursive or Manuscript

You'll be the one to decide whether your students can write using manuscript or whether they must practice cursive during this time. Children should not have to wonder and worry; they should know what you expect and why. Remember that the purpose of the writing time is to learn how to get ideas on paper. Revision and editing time is when to make it better and worry about spelling, grammar, etc. Many teachers let students do what is most comfortable and legible (you will have to be able to read it!) when drafting and then demand that the final copy is either in their best handwriting or typed.

Margins

If your students are using notebook paper or notebooks, then you need to explain about margins and your expectations—margins on one side or two? If you are passing out plain paper or if students are printing pages, what kind of margins do you expect? Using margins may be new to some students, so be sure to let them know what to do and why.

Keeping EVERYTHING

Because writing every day shows the growth of the writer, ask your students to keep everything they write. You will need to determine how often you will collect drafts that have not been published and possibly store them outside of the writing folder for the student. However, you want students to keep everything. All of the drafts and pages students revise and edit need to be connected to the actual published pieces. Each page shows a step in the process. The writing folders or notebooks will get clogged if the students are left to handle all papers from the beginning of the year to the end. For that reason, you may want to establish days (once a quarter? once every mid-quarter?) when you will gather any papers your students want to relinquish. Then, you will need to decide how to store those papers, so that at the end of the year, all pieces are returned to the students. Many students then prepare a portfolio of their writing for the year.

You may also have requests from parents to view some of this writing. The writing folders are not sent home for obvious reasons. You will decide whether you will send original published pieces for viewing and keep photocopies or just the opposite.

Mini-Lesson Focus: Creating a Writing Handbook (Procedures)

For older students, it is certainly acceptable to expect them to be a bit more responsible for their own learning during mini-lessons. The time you spend on mini-lessons is invaluable—it is your instruction. Students in fourth grade and beyond can be expected to take notes, create examples, and refer to the examples later on. Ask each student to bring a spiral notebook or a composition notebook to each mini-lesson. Nancie Atwell (1998) and Linda Rief (1992) both suggest this way of creating a handbook for referencing. Your job will be to think through what should be written each day.

The teacher says:

"Each of you has brought a notebook in as one of your supplies. That notebook will be used each day during our writing mini-lesson. I've asked each of you to bring your notebook to our mini-lesson today. On the top of the very first page, I want you to write the title: Table of Contents. You are going to be leaving the first three pages of your notebook blank for now. As you begin to take notes and create some examples, we will go back to these three blank pages and write in our Table of Contents. This notebook will be a tool for you. You will need to spend time making it a tool you can use.

"Go ahead and skip those three pages. At the bottom right hand corner of the fourth page, write the number one. You will be numbering the pages in your handbook just like a book. This way you can refer back to things easily. These notebooks will also help us if someone is absent. I can ask a student to meet with the person who was absent and share the notes from the day or days he was gone.

"Many times when I am conferencing with you, I will ask you to bring your notebook along. It will only be helpful if you have it with you and use it whenever you need to. These notebooks stay in our classroom. The only writing you will do in them will be during mini-lesson time, and they are going to be important tools, so I don't want you to take them home.

"These are not notebooks for your actual pieces of writing. You will be using your folders (or whatever you have chosen to use) for that. These notebooks are only for mini-lesson time. Please, make sure yours is labeled clearly, you have Table of Contents at the top of the first page, and you've numbered the first ten pages we'll use to take notes."

Procedures mini-lessons don't take long, but they are critical to making the routines in your Writing Block run smoothly. As you develop and plan mini-lessons, decide what a student would write down when you are finished. If you and the class make a list of criteria together, it is easy to have them copy down the list. However, if your lesson is a time when they watch you write something, make sure at the end of the lesson you indicate if nothing should be written or give them a one- or two-sentence summary of what they were learning. There are also times when you may want to type a list of things or give the students a paper you've copied to trim and glue or tape into their notebooks. Your decisions about what will be included should also help them in the process of making these useful.

Mini-Lesson Focus: Author's Chair (Procedures)

Early in the year, sharing in the upper grades may be very informal. You might call the children together after they write and let several of your students tell you what they are writing about. Students will soon realize that each day "the teacher does a mini-lesson then I write." When you think your students are ready, you can begin your formal sharing or Author's Chair. In Author's Chair, students share one piece of writing, and then ask the other students to make comments ("Say something nice" is a rule!) and ask questions. Most teachers designate $1/5$ of the class to share each day. Many teachers use a special chair (rocking chair, big stuffed chair, decorated plastic chair, etc.) for this—or even a stool will do! You can introduce Author's Chair to your students in a mini-lesson; you can write about Writer's Workshop—what you will do each day and why.

The teacher talks about the class's daily writing time as she writes:

"Today, I am going to write about what we do every day during Writer's Workshop. Every day, I talk and I write; we call this our mini-lesson. During the mini-lesson, I talk about writing and how writers write, and what they think about and do. I talk about something you need to learn to become better writers. I write something so you can see what I want you to do as you write.

"Every day, we talk about writing, and I write for you. We call this our mini-lesson. A mini-lesson focuses on something we need to learn to become better writers.

"After I write, it is your turn to write. You return to your seats, get your writing folders (or notebooks) and begin to write. What do I do while you are writing? Yes, I will walk around the room (or call you to my desk or a special table) and conference with some of you. We talk about what you are writing about.

"As you write, I conference with some students each day. We talk about what you have written and what you plan to do next. I tell you what I like about your writing. Sometimes we talk about ways to improve your writing.

"Usually we end our writing time by sharing our writing. Starting today, we will use this chair (shows the Author's Chair). Everyone will be assigned a certain day each week to share. I have made a class schedule for sharing." (The schedule has days one through five and $1/5$ of the students' names are written after each day.) "On your day, you sit in our Author's Chair and read something you have written since your last sharing turn. The writing could be a work in progress, something you have finished, or something you have published and want to share.

"We will start Author's Chair today, so if your name is after day one (reads the names), look through your folders (or notebooks), find a piece you want to read, and get ready to share. Today, I will conference with those who will share today. You can read your piece to me, and we will talk about it and get ready for Author's Chair."

After the students have written and the teacher has spent two to three minutes with each child who will share today, it is time for the first Author's Chair.

It is also time for the teacher to model some "nice" comments ("I liked your story about hiking in the mountains. It sounds like a beautiful place.").

Then, she asks the first question ("How did you find out about this hiking trail?").

Mini-Lesson Focus: Using a Think-Aloud for Beginning Capitalization and Ending Punctuation (Conventions)

In the upper grades, students should be held accountable for the correct use of capital letters and ending punctuation. By this time, students have had instruction in using capital letters at the beginnings of sentences and using the correct punctuation marks at the ends of sentences. This lesson will focus on how writers begin every sentence with a capital letter and end every sentence with a period, question mark, or exclamation point.

The teacher talks about what she will write about and says:

"I am going to write about my trip to see my sister in Sedona, Arizona today. I will tell you who went on this trip with me and what I did while I was there. However, the focus today is remembering and reminding you that all sentences start with capital letters and end with correct punctuation. You all know that. The trick is to remember to use it when you are busy writing and your mind is on telling something, not on beginning capitals and ending punctuation." (As you talk and write make a mistake or two that you can correct during your quick edit that you will do with your class immediately after writing.)

The teacher talks and writes:

My Trip to Sedona, Arizona

("I must remember that titles need capital letters, too. I remember to start each sentence with a capital letter.") In October, I flew to Phoenix, Arizona, with my daughter, Suzanne. ("I remember to put a period at the end of the first sentence and start the second sentence with a capital letter.") There, we met my mother who had flown in from Massachusetts, where she lives. ("I remember to put a period at the end of that sentence and start the next sentence with a capital letter.") We rented a car, and I drove to Sedona. Do you know where that is? ("Since that is a question, I need to put a question mark at the end of that sentence.") Sedona is 100 miles north of Phoenix, Arizona. As you enter the city, you see red rock mountains. What a beautiful sight! ("I remember to put an exclamation point at the end of that sentence. I start the next sentence with a capital letter.") My sister, Kathy, lives in Oak Creek Canyon. Each time I visit my sister I am always amazed; it is such an amazing place. There are many places to see you can drive or you can hike where you want to go. Since I was driving, my sister made sure that we went past all of the famous spots.

The teacher does a quick edit with the class:

She reads each sentence and checks for a capital letter at the beginning and the correct punctuation at the end. She decides that she had gotten so busy telling about Sedona that she forgot to put a period at the end of the sentence: There are many places to see. The teacher also needs a capital letter for the start of the next sentence: You can drive or you can hike where you want to go. She reminds the students that daily quick edits help her do her best when writing.

As the students go to write, the teacher reminds them that they are responsible for using capital letters at the beginning and correct punctuation at the end of each sentence.

Other Ideas for Beginning Capitalization and Ending Punctuation

Focusing on Capital Letters at the Beginnings of Sentences

If your students are frequently forgetting capital letters at the beginnings of sentences, then you need to do a lesson that just focuses on that. Begin to write and remind the students that each time you start a sentence you need to begin with a capital letter.

In October, I went to the Grand Canyon with my daughter, my sister, and my mother. (I started my first sentence with a capital letter because all sentences start that way. My next sentence also begins with a capital letter.) We drove to . . . .

Writing a Piece with No Capital Letters at the Beginnings of Sentences and Correcting It

Before class, write a piece and do not begin any sentences with capitals. Talk about how hard it is to read writing like this. Then, let a volunteer student using a red (or any other color) pen, correct your writing, or you can correct the writing with the class's help.

My Trip to the Grand Canyon

in October, I went to the Grand Canyon with my daughter, my sister, and my mother. my mother and I had been to the Grand Canyon before; my daughter had not. we drove along the southern wall of the canyon from west to east. there were many places to stop, park, and look out over the canyon. each stop offered a breathtaking view. we took pictures, but we could not get everything we wanted into view. the Grand Canyon is a beautiful sight to see!

Focusing on "Telling Sentences" and Exclamations

Remind your students that periods are used at the ends of sentences that make statements ("tells you something") or give a command that is not an exclamation. When a reader comes to a period, it is a signal to stop. Write a piece with lots of "telling sentences." After your quick edit, you can remind the class that most of the sentences were statements or "telling sentences" and needed periods at the ends. Which two sentences needed exclamation points? Why?

Autumn

Autumn is another name for fall. I like autumn in North Carolina. I like to see the leaves turn red, yellow, and orange. Driving down some streets you can see some beautiful fall sights! Besides the colorful leaves, you can see pumpkins and cornstalks in many yards. There are fairs and festivals in many small towns and in some big cities. The weather gets cooler, and we have to wear our warmer clothes. The only thing I don't like is raking leaves!

Focusing on Questions and Question Marks

Write a piece with lots of questions. After your quick edit, you can remind the class that most of the sentences were questions and needed question marks at the ends.

The World Series

At the end of the baseball season, the World Series is played. Have you ever watched the World Series? What two teams played? Which team was your favorite? Did they win? Who was your favorite player? What do you remember most about the games?

Mini-Lesson Focus: What to Do about Spelling (Procedures/Conventions)

In most classrooms, the students are learning so much about writing that they need constant reminders of things they have learned earlier. One of those areas in which upper-grades students need constant reminders is spelling. Many students think the only resources that are available are the teacher and the dictionary. Neither of these options is a good solution during writing. If you have to stop for every student who can't spell a word, your time will be totally consumed. Also, the rough draft stage is not the time to consult a dictionary, and your students need to know that. Dictionaries are used during editing, not writing. What will you teach them about spelling? Teach them to use word wall words and spell those words correctly. Teach them to look at bulletin boards and words in the room from the themes and subjects you are studying and use those words. Also, teach them to do what adults do when they cannot spell a word—stretch it out and write the letters that represent the sounds they hear.

For this lesson, you will choose any subject—yourself, family, pets, hobbies, or any area of the curriculum. Plan your lesson so that there will be several words with spellings that might be unfamiliar to many of your students. When you get to these words, you will model for your students what you would do and why.

The teacher says:

"We have been reading about Canada. Today, I am going to begin a summary of some things we have read. I will show you what I do when I come to words I am not sure how to spell."

Canada

Canada is the northern neighbor ("That is a word wall word, so I look on the word wall to write **neighbor** correctly.") of the United States. There were many aborijinal (stretches out **ab-or-ij-in-al**, circles it) people living in Canada when the first settlers arived (stretches out **a-rived**, circles it) in the 16th century (stretches out **cen-tur-e** and says, "I hear an **e** at the end of that word, but I know that it is a **y**."). In 1534, Jacques Cartier ("His name is on our bulletin board of Canada settlers, so I look over there to make sure I spell both his first and last names correctly.") first settled Quebec ("I can find the spelling of **Quebec** on the same bulletin board.") for France. Even today, more than 80 percent of the people in Quebec list French as their first language.

Another early settler was . . . .

It may take you two or three days of mini-lessons to write a summary or story. Each day the teacher focuses on spelling words her students may find difficult to spell until students understand what they are to do and how the word wall and other words in the room are resources to help them with spelling. When they don't know how to spell a word and can't find it in the room, then they stretch it out, spell it as best they can, and circle it.

The teacher remembers to tell her students, "After I stretch out the sounds and write the word, I always circle it. That way I'll remember to check it later, if I work on this piece again and take it through the writing process." (You will not believe how much circling words will help some students, especially those hung-up on correctness. The circling seems to give them permission to continue writing and let you know they know that it wasn't spelled right.)

Other Ideas for What to Do about Spelling

Spelling by Stretching, Circling, and Using Proofreader's Marks

If you wish to teach your students how to use proofreader's marks (and many upper-grades teachers do) you can model circling the misspelled word and writing **sp** above the circle. Write a piece modeling how you stretch and circle words when you are not sure of the spelling. Then, write **sp** above each circled word.

Anne of Green Gables

Anne of Green Gables is a famous (Canadean) [sp] (stretches out **Ca-na-de-an**, circles it) book written for children. The author was Lucy Maud Montgomery. She wrote the book a long time ago, in 1908. It is a story about an (orfan) [sp] (stretches out **or-fan**, circles it) girl named Anne who was adopted by Matthew and Marilla Culbert. The Culberts wanted to adopt a boy to help with the chores. Instead, they got a red-headed girl who they soon came to love. Anne . . . .

Looking at First Drafts of Students' Writing

Have each student write a summary of a book he is reading or a response to a prompt in the content areas. (For example, describe the three regions of North Carolina.) Save an example with no name on it, make a transparency, and proofread it with your students. See if the writer remembered what to do about spelling as he wrote this piece:

North Carolina

North Carolina has three regions (on bulletin board in room): the coast (on bulletin board in room), the piedmont (on bulletin board in room), and the mountains (on bulletin board in room). The coast is known for (torism) [sp] (stretches out, circles, and puts "sp" over it) It has many beaches. Crops like cotton and peanuts are grown on the flat lands of the coast. (on bulletin board in room)

The piedmont plateau (on bulletin board in room), is known for manufacturing (stretches out the word and spells it correctly). Many companies . . . .

Editing for Spelling

Take a piece of writing (your writing or a student's writing with no name on it) and show students how you would edit the piece and correct the spellings with use of the dictionary and the content area book, if necessary, to find the correct spelling of some words.

Mini-Lesson Focus: Editing Your Writing with a Writer's Checklist (Procedures/Conventions)

As in previous grades, students will need to be held accountable for items on a Writer's Checklist. The items placed on the list are those concepts/skills you feel your students have had enough instruction in and exposure to, to be accountable for self-assessment. The checklist will include concepts of revision and editing. The balance is important. If students are held accountable only for editing, they may interpret that to mean that editing is more important than content. The opposite could also be true. Therefore, the lists should include both. In the lower grades, teachers add one item at a time. To begin your upper-grades checklist, start with three items on this first day. The other items on the checklist will be added one at a time. (We've chosen to begin with items we feel have been well taught prior to fourth grade.)

The teacher says:

"Each year, you have had a checklist to guide you as you begin to publish a piece of writing. We will have a checklist this year, too. Most of the time, we will add one item to the list at a time. However, today we are going to begin our checklist with three items. I think you are all old enough and know how to use these writing rules. So for today, we will begin our Writer's Checklist with three familiar items.

"The first thing on our checklist goes along with the procedure we learned just the other day. I want you all to make sure you have written your name and date on each piece of writing. So number one on our checklist says 'I have included my name and the date.' You know that, in this class, I want it written in the upper right-hand corner (or wherever you want this).

"For the second item, I would like for someone to tell me what you know about the kind of letters we use to begin sentences (asks for a response from the students). Great, it is important that each of you not only know what kind of letter to begin a sentence with, but that you check to make sure you've done it. What do you all know about ending a sentence (asks for a response from the students)? Right, there has to be some kind of ending punctuation. It might be a period, a question mark, or an exclamation point. Be sure to choose the type of punctuation needed by your sentence, and use it! So, number two on our checklist is, 'I have used beginning capitals and correct ending punctuation.'

"The last thing we'll add to our checklist today deals with spelling. We need to check our writing to see if we have all words spelled correctly. If we spelled it the best we could or stretched it out to spell it, then you might want to check that word when editing. So, number three is 'I have circled suspect words.'

"As I write these on our checklist today, I will add today's date to the side. Now, we all know that from this day on, you are each responsible for checking your own writing for these items."

> Writer's Checklist
>
> 1. I have included my name and the date. (9/16/02)
>
> 2. I have used beginning capitals and correct ending punctuation. (9/16/02)
>
> 3. I have circled suspect words. (9/16/02)

As the year progresses, the teacher will need to add to the Writer's Checklist. If it is to be a manageable tool, the number of items on the list should not exceed 10 (if some items have more than one thing for students to look at) or 15 (if each item is put on separately). Students will certainly be taught many more things than those that appear on the checklist. (Choose carefully what you will add, as these should be concepts the students can apply and edit for in their own writing.)

The teacher will create this checklist to be posted in the classroom. However, these students are old enough to also be keeping track of the items on the checklist in their own writing folders or their Writer's Handbook. They need to learn to edit at home as well as school.

Other Ideas for Editing

Being Sure All Sentences Make Sense and Stay on Topic

(Whether you add these separately or together depends on your class.) Students need to get in the habit of reading their writing aloud to themselves and to others. Our brains tend to insert words and phrases that are not on the page when we reread our writing to ourselves. It is critical that the sentences make sense to the reader and that they are about the topic. Often, if an author forgets to read it aloud, it only makes sense to the author. Write a short paragraph or the beginning of a story and purposely omit words and phrases. Confuse common words (for example, what for want, etc.). Add a sentence that is not on topic. Read it to your students and ask them to help you make some changes. For a bit of guided practice, have each student take out a piece of writing, read a section of it to a partner, and listen for sentences that make sense and stay on topic.

Spelling Word Wall Words Correctly

Some classes may need this lesson before number three on the Writer's Checklist. Once you have begun to add words to your word wall, either word wall words or Nifty Thrifty Fifty words, students are expected to use those words correctly. These are not words the teacher should have to help edit. Students should write them correctly the first time, every time. If a word is misspelled, it should be the student's responsibility to fix the word. As the year progresses, your support lessens. The teacher may begin by pointing out the words for students to fix, progress to indicating a line of print where a misspelled word wall word occurs, and then finally, state that student papers are not accepted with misspelled word wall words. Asking students to fix the problems often has a greater impact than just taking points off. To add this to the checklist, have your students help you find misspelled word wall words in a piece of writing you present.

Circling Words You Are Unsure Of

In some classes early in the year, you will also want to give students a procedure for dealing with those words they are not sure of. Problems occur if the teacher begins spelling all of the words asked by students, just as problems occur if students are expected to look up each word they don't know. It is important for students to attempt spelling a word using strategies they learn during word work. It is also important to keep moving with any ideas you have during writing time. Looking up each word can interrupt the flow of ideas. Encouraging students to write the words the way they think they should be spelled and circle the word to indicate that it is one to pay attention to during the publishing process, allows students to keep moving with their writing. It is, however, also a way to say to students that spelling does matter.

Mini-Lesson Focus: Making Decisions about What to Write (Craft)

As students begin to write, they will make decisions about the genre best suited for the topic. In other words, not everything on their writing lists should be a story. Sometimes a writer doesn't know what genre best suits the topic without trying, and sometimes there is a natural fit. Use this mini-lesson to model how you've made some genre decisions about certain topics on your Writing List. Remind students that the decision is not always obvious, but the reason you've created a list of different kinds of writing is because not everything is a story.

The teacher thinks aloud:

"I want to go back to my writing list today and show you some other decisions I've made. Earlier, I wrote about Merrill Kaye being chased by the Canada geese and wrote it in a story (or narrative—use the language your students are familiar with). As I look over my list, I told you that I wrote about Jeff in a journal on a scrapbook page. See, as I thought about that idea, I really didn't have enough to make a story. There wasn't a problem and solution, but it was something I wanted to write about and remember. I might call that an anecdote; have you ever seen anecdotes in the *Reader's Digest*?

"I also told you I had written about my mother's 'laughing brown eyes.' As I thought about that topic, that particular line sounded like a line out of a poem to me, and I started thinking about other things associated with my mother's eyes. But in my opinion, 'laughing brown eyes' wouldn't have made a good story, so I chose to write a poem.

"As I look at other ideas on my list, I can see other kinds of writing. For example, sometimes I want to make a list of all the foods I remember being my favorites at Ma-ma's. That would be a list, not a poem, or a story.

"Remember that as you choose the topic to write on, you've only made part of your decision. The next decision will be what genre would best suit the topic. You might have to try more than one genre before you decide what is best."

The teacher then sends the students to write. As she begins conferencing, this mini-lesson may be referred to occasionally. More than likely, she will have at least one person who prefers writing expository or nonfiction writing. She models both fiction and nonfiction examples.

(Some students will assume that all writing must be in story form. Help them move beyond that assumption, if another genre would be less cumbersome or threatening for them.)

My Writing Ideas	
Jeff	the night we met at Singsations tryouts
	hearing him sing "The Lord's Prayer"
	"Daddy is a handsome man, doo-dah"
	✔The changes in him since we moved
Merrill Kaye	her love of books
	the talking trash can at Disney World
	being chased by wild geese
Alex	the perfectionist
	becoming an artist, its ups and downs
	collecting the poison ivy
Lafe	swimming in the "cat pool"
	"It's just what boys do!"
	my little sugar bear
Mother	how I miss her
	✔her laughing brown eyes
	her ability to express herself
Ma-ma	the last jar of raspberry jelly
	a list of my favorite foods
	no time to mourn
Teaching	watching the "light bulb come on"
	adults are my new students
Professional life	working on a book of mini-lessons for upper grades

Other Ideas for Making Decisions about What to Write

Doing Some Expository Writing

If someone in the class has a writing list that better reflects expository writing, ask if you could use some examples and talk about how some could be articles, essays, or informational pieces. Or, make sure some of the items on your list make a good connection to the nonfiction part of writing.

Using Topics from Social Studies

Add ideas tied to your social studies units to your writing list. For example, writing about life in North Carolina during the Revolutionary War or Civil War, watching Wilbur and Orville Wright flying the first airplane on the Outer Banks, etc. Would a journal or diary piece be better than an informational article? When studying the Appalachian Mountains, the Ozark Mountains, or life in Mexico or Canada, etc., you can model how to write and illustrate a brochure about the area. It could include the history as well as the geography and facts about that area today. As students learn more, they have more to write about! Some students enjoy writing about people, places, and things they are learning about. One student wrote "Twenty-Five Things I Have Learned about North Carolina" and caused a classroom of students to want to write the same!

Using Topics from Science

Many students would rather write about things they find interesting—hurricanes, electricity, rocks, the life cycle of moths, etc. They would rather read about tornadoes during self-selected reading or when they have free time, then write about the many things they learned about tornadoes. As you study about new things in science, remind students that they can write about these new topics also.

Using Fiction Books as Models

When reading a story, whether it is a picture book or chapter book, some students might like to use that book as a springboard to writing. *The True Story of the Three Pigs* by Jon Scieszka (Viking Penguin, 1989) can lead students to writing other stories they have read from another character's point of view (for example: *The True Story of Cinderella*, from the stepmother's point of view; *The True Story of Little Read Riding Hood*, from the wolf's point of view; *The True Story of the Gingerbread Man*, from his point of view; *The True Story of Harry Potter*, from his cousin's point of view, etc.). Did you know *Captain Underpants* was thought of and written by Dav Pilkey (Scholastic Inc., 1977) when he was a student in elementary school? Some students, especially at this age, love to use their imaginations instead of telling us about their lives!

Writing Poetry

When reading poetry during a teacher read-aloud or Guided Reading, you can remind your students that they, too, can write poetry. There are always a few children who find poetry fascinating and can do a good job mimicking the poetry they read. These same students often write some wonderful poetry of their own.

Mini-Lesson Focus: Different Writing Genres (Craft)

Just as you expose and encourage your students to read many kinds of texts, you want them to know about and try many types of writing. Some students may think the writing they do in school is limited to "stories, reports, and letters." It seems that these are very common genres for schools. However, the Writing Block is a time to allow students to find their own niches in the writing genres most comfortable to them. Use a mini-lesson to chart the many types of writing your students can imagine.

The teacher says:

"Today, I want you to help me make a chart. I want us to think together and list all of the different ways or different things that can be written. We are going to keep this chart and post it here in the room. We also want to add to it as the year goes on. It may help you make better writing decisions during your writing time. So, what are some things we can write?"

"When we've been reading different types of books, we've noticed what genre the book is. As I read aloud to you, I've tried to read to you from many different genres. In writing, we also call these different categories genres. Remember, if you think of another writing or genre, let me know, and we'll include it. I know we'll collect more before the year is over."

Different Writing Genres

* Story	* Information
* Letter	* Persuasive
* Poem	* Advertisement
* Song	* Editorial
* Note	* Comic strip
* Report	* Announcement
* Article	* Invitation
* Cartoon	* Science fiction
* Play	* Tall tale
* Anecdote	* Fable
* Biography	* Fairy tale
* Autobiography	* Weather forecast
* Joke	* Comparison
* Essay	* Narrative
* How to	* Expository
* Memoir	* Recipe

The examples on this chart are just that. Some would even represent similar genres. For example, a report, an article, or information would all be expository texts. (Your students will determine how it is written on the chart. They will call it the term they are familiar with.) As the teacher continues through the year, if he would like to refine their categories, he has another mini-lesson. (Because you are dealing with older students, not only will this be posted in the classroom, but you should also give students copies of this list and expect them to keep lists in their writing folders to refer to.)

Other Ideas for Different Writing Genres

Creating a File of Examples

In order to write a particular genre, an author needs examples to fall back on. For this reason, it would be helpful if you create a file of examples from some of the less well-known genres. For example, some of your students may have never seen an essay, a book review, or a movie review. If you refer to anecdotes, you'll want to provide examples. The easiest way to create this file, is to use a crate to house hanging files (Atwell, 1998). In the crate, create a file for each genre you want to find examples for. Then, as you discover or read those examples, photocopy them and place in your file. For example, news magazines such as *Time* and *Newsweek* have weekly essays. These are good examples for your students. *Reader's Digest* often publishes anecdotes. Most newspapers and magazines have regular book reviews and movie reviews.

Once you've created this filing system, take one mini-lesson to demonstrate its purpose and where students can find it. It would also be helpful to collect sample papers from students each year to add to your file. Remove names from the papers, even if you have the students' permission.

Writing the Genre You Are Reading

When reading aloud to your students or discussing a genre during Guided Reading, use your mini-lesson time to model for your students how they, too, can write a mystery, short story, picture book, poem, play, or informational article.

Writing a Comparison

Compare two stories (or books), use a Venn diagram, and write a comparison piece. Compare two parts of your state (or province), two parts of your country, or two cities; then use a Venn diagram and write a comparison. You could also compare two things you studied in science and write a comparison. This is a perfect genre to integrate writing with subject matter.

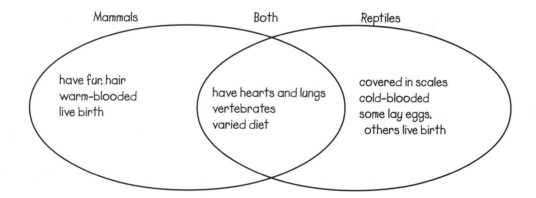

Mammals — have fur, hair, warm-blooded, live birth

Both — have hearts and lungs, vertebrates, varied diet

Reptiles — covered in scales, cold-blooded, some lay eggs, others live birth

Writing a Weather Report

If weather is a topic in your curriculum this year, writing a weather report is something you can do with your class. Many students find this easy (and fun!) to write.

Mini-Lesson Focus: Sentences that Make Sense and Stay on Topic (Procedures/Craft)

Each student should be in the habit of checking to see if his writing has his name and the date and if all of his sentences begin with capital letters and end with the correct punctuation. He should also be circling words he thinks are misspelled. Once students are in the habit of doing these things, it is time to add another item to your Writer's Checklist: all sentences make sense and stay on topic. (This can be two items if you have a class that would benefit from adding each item separately.) Students, even in the upper grades, think all of their sentences make sense. They usually read what they wanted to write, not what they have written. That is why peer editing often helps so much after self-editing and why the teacher needs to be the final editor on published pieces.

The teacher says:

"People who check writing are called editors. Soon, we will start self-editing and peer editing the writing we do in class. We have started to do some self-editing with a Writer's Checklist, so you know to check for capital letters at the beginning of each sentence and the correct punctuation at the end of each sentence. You also know what to do when you cannot spell a word and how to circle that word (and write "sp"?) when you know that the word is not spelled correctly. Today, we are going to add something new to our list, but it is something you have heard for many years: all sentences make sense and stay on topic. I want you to watch me write and then check to see if all of the sentences I write make sense and stay on topic."

The teacher talks and writes:

Ice Hockey

Ice hockey is played in the winter months. It is a favorite for people living in Canada. and the northern regions of the United States. The game is played on frozen ponds, on roads, and in ice rinks. The players use hockey sticks to hit the puck. The goalie skates in front of the net and tries to stop the shots. There is also a professional hockey league. called the National Hockey League (NHL). Many people like basketball better than hockey. Some of the greatest hockey players are Wayne Gretzky, Mario Lemieux, Bobby Orr, and Gordie Howe.

The students read each sentence and indicate (thumbs up or thumbs down) whether each sentence makes sense and stays on topic.

The sentences that do not make sense are combined so that they do make sense, and the changes are made on the transparency or board.

It is a favorite for people living in Canada and the northern regions of the United States.

There is also a professional hockey league called the National Hockey League (NHL).

The sentence that does not stay on topic (Many people like basketball better than hockey.) is crossed out and the teacher explains that the sentence does makes sense but does not add to the writing and is not needed.

Add to the Writer's Checklist

4. I have used sentences that make sense and stay on topic.

Other Ideas for Sentences that Make Sense and Stay on Topic

Providing a Definition of a Sentence

In the upper grades, students might want a definition of a sentence, since they are often given definitions for vocabulary words in their reading, social studies, science, and math text books. Here is one definition of a sentence, "A group of words expressing a complete thought and possessing a subject and predicate." The subject is usually a noun or pronoun. The predicate usually has a verb in it. If you want to work on sentences using this definition, then you might take a piece of writing you have written on the overhead and find the subject and predicate in each sentence.

Combining Short Sentences

Sentences that make a strong point or call for an action are shorter and more direct. Many short sentences in one piece probably indicate the need for some sentence combining. Write a piece with many short sentences (or save one from a former class—no name!) and make an overhead transparency. Use this transparency to combine sentences.

> I went to the mall. I went with Suzanne. We shopped. We went to all of the big department stores. She was looking for a new dress. She bought one. It was black.

This would sound better if some sentences were combined.

> I went to the mall with Suzanne. We shopped in all of the big department stores. She was looking for a new black dress. She found one!

Finding Long Sentences that Might Be Run-On Sentences

Sentences that are too long do not give the reader time to rest. Write a piece with run-on sentences (or save one from a former class—no name!) and make an overhead transparency. Use this transparency to find and change run-on sentences.

> It is hard to tell how the idea first entered my head but once it was conceived it haunted me day and night all I could think about was writing a book about my winning game. I wanted to write that book and I did not have time because each day I had to go to school, to soccer practice, and then did my homework still all I could think about was writing the story of my winning game.

This would sound better if the run-on sentences were replaced.

> It was hard to tell how the idea first entered my head, but once it was conceived, it haunted me day and night. All I could think about was writing a book about my winning game. I wanted to write that book. I did not have time because each day I had to go to school, to soccer practice, and then did my homework. Still, all I could think about was writing the story of my winning game.

Mini-Lesson Focus: The Writing Process (Procedures)

In the primary grades, students often learn to write, edit their mistakes, and then publish. Starting in the upper grades, students need to learn that there is more to the writing process than just looking for "mistakes."

Discuss what writers do as they write for publication. Write the steps on a large piece of chart paper or on a transparency and have your students add it to their writing handbooks. Some teachers post this chart early in the year but expect their students, after having gone through this process a number of times, to know this information without using the chart later in the year. Students who haven't learned the process yet can open their writing handbooks and see just what they need to do next. Students need to know that writers go through a process that looks like this.

The teacher says:

"Each day, you write. Some days, you write about topics you choose. Other days, you write in response to something we have studied in social studies or science. Your writing is looking good, and I think you are ready to start thinking about the writing process as authors do when they write. Not everything you write in school is going to be published, but sometimes you will write such a good piece that you will want to share it with the class and show it to others, or publish it. When you want to make your writing public, you take a closer look at it and take some extra steps. I am not talking about the quick edit we sometimes do. I am talking about taking some steps to grow as writers and to make sure that what you show others is truly your best work." (takes a piece of chart paper or a transparency to use with the overhead projector)

"This is what I do when I write. First, I find a topic (writes 'find a topic') I think I would like to write about. It is easier for me to write about my family, friends, or teaching, than it is for me to write fiction and make up a story. Sometimes I prewrite and outline or make a list of things I want to remember to include in my writing, then I write (writes 'write'). After writing for a while, I always have to read what I have written and see if I am saying what I want to say and including everything I want to (writes 'read/revise')."

WRITERS:

* find a topic

* write

* read/revise

* rework, add on

* read again, decide if content is right

* self-edit

* peer edit

* teacher edits

* go public or publish

"That is why every time I do a mini-lesson and continue to write, I always read what I have before I start to write again (writes 'rework, add on'). When I think I am finished, I read it one more time to see if I got the content right—did I include everything I wanted to write? (writes 'read again, decide if content is right') Then, I do a check for grammar, spelling, and mechanics (writes 'self-edit'). You can use your Writer's Checklist in your writing workbook to do your self-editing; that's what it is for. When my writing is about as good as I can do, I always like someone else to look at it (writes 'peer edit'). Sometimes I send it to Amanda, Karen, or Deb and ask them what they think—did I leave anything important out? Then, I send it off to my editor, Joey. He makes sure I get it absolutely right before it is published. I will be your editor and make sure your work is right before you publish it (writes 'teacher edits,' then 'go public or publish').

"Today, I want you to look through your writing and see if you find something that you wrote that you especially like. I will ask you about this as I conference this week. What have you written that you think is your best work? Are there two or three good selections? If so, you will have to choose which one to take through the writing process."

Other Ideas for the Writing Process

Modeling the New Cycle of Writing with Your Students

Spend a week or two modeling this cycle with your students. Select a topic from your list (or use the writing you did with one of the first lessons on "Modeling How to Write Using a Think-Aloud" or "Prewriting Using a Think-Aloud.") Pinpoint something about the piece you select that you can work on, add on to, revise, or further develop. Make a few "mistakes" or omissions so that you can really use the writer's checklist. Do all of this work in front of the students as you think aloud and make decisions that writers make about their work. Then, ask either the class as a whole or one student in particular to be your "peer editor." Ask what they want to know more about, etc.

Making a Class Book of Short Stories after Reading and Learning about this Type of Fiction

This will give the class a real reason to take pieces through the writing process.

Making a Class Book about Any Subject You Are Studying in the Content Areas

Do not have your students go through this publishing process if you are the only one to read their work.

Making a Bulletin Board or Display in the Hall to "Make Public" Your Published Pieces

Publishing gives students a reason to write and take their writing through the writing process!

Mini-Lesson Focus: Self-Editing and Peer Editing (Procedures)

In the upper grades, the first editor of any piece should be the writer, and the first focus should be on content. Once the writer says what he wants to say, then mechanical issues can be addressed. The writer needs to make some decisions when self-editing. What are the strengths of this piece, or what is good? What are the weaknesses of this piece, or what needs more work? Once the students understand the importance of what they are trying to say as writers, then they also begin to care about how the words are written, therefore the need for them to edit. Self-editing is a skill that some students enjoy—for others it is hard work. Peer editing is also easier for some students than others, and having a Writer's Checklist helps with both tasks.

The teacher says:

"When you have written a good piece and want others to read your writing, it needs to be revised and edited first. The first editor of any piece of writing is always the writer. He reads the piece to himself, at least once (and probably more than once) and reworks those parts he thinks could be improved. Good writers spend a lot of time reading over and thinking about what they have written. Then, they look at the writing to see if it is grammatically correct and has the correct punctuation. We have been using a Writer's Checklist to do quick edits, so now we will take more time and make sure we have everything just like we should. I have chosen a piece I wrote before, and I will edit it for you; then you, as a class, will become my peer editors and look at it again."

The teacher puts some writing on a transparency and begins to talk about her piece:

Merrill Kaye trudged along the dam at the edge of the lake. Dusk was approaching and she was ready to head back to the house. Not far from the edge of the bank, close to the tall grass, she saw Momma Goose and Daddy Goose. For the past month, Merrill Kaye had been watching the geese take care of the babies. She knew they were pretty protective, and the babies always obeyed their parents. As she walked past the parents, Merrill Kaye noticed she had come between them and their babies. Momma and Daddy began to feel threatened and separated.

As I watched out the kitchen window, I saw Momma and Daddy Goose running after Merrill Kaye; their necks outstretched, hissing through their beaks, and running as fast as they could. Merrill Kaye was running, too, looking over her shoulder with a fearful face. Just as she got to the edge of the tall grass she tripped and fell. Luckily, the geese felt she was now far enough away, and they hurried back to the young geese.

I ran out the back door and saw Merrill Kaye smiling and laughing as she made it back up to the house. I knew her expression would have been different if the geese had caught up with her. Fortunately, they didn't, and our memory of the story is told with laughter even three years later.

"I think I could make this story better by doing a better job of 'setting the stage.' My lead needs a little work. What if I tried this:

The sun was setting, and a rainbow of colors reflected in the water of our small lake. I looked out the window as I washed the dishes from dinner.

"Now, I think I'll go back to the way I began the story, but the second sentence needs to be changed.

> The sun was setting, and a rainbow of colors reflected in the water of our small lake. I looked out the window as I washed the dishes from dinner. Merrill Kaye trudged along the dam at the edge of the lake. ~~Dusk was approaching and~~ As dusk approached, she was ready to head back to the house. Not far from the edge of the bank, close to the tall grass, she saw Momma Goose and Daddy Goose.

"Next, I check for capital letters and a punctuation mark at the end of each sentence. Then, I check for misspelled words; any words that I have circled, I check in the dictionary. All of my sentences make sense and stay on topic. I'm done."

Other Ideas for Self-Editing and Peer Editing

Doing a Class Edit of a Student's Writing

Let a student with a finished piece revise that piece with the class's help. Talk about what the student has written. What could she add or change to make it better? Have the class use the checklist to edit the writing just as they did with your writing. You can also do this by selecting a piece of writing from a previous class—no name—to use on the overhead. Again, allow students to assist you in revising and editing the piece.

Doing Lots of Lessons in which You Choose Someone to be Your Editing Partner

The best way to teach peer editing is to let your students edit your writing and their classmates' writing. Even students in the upper grades like to get a red pen and become your editing partner. Choose some of your "natural editors" to do this job as everyone watches. Some teachers buy a special visor and write "Editor" across the front of the visor with a black marker. Be sure to express your appreciation for the student's help in making your piece much more readable. Peer editing will help them see that editing is not "looking for what is wrong" but helping someone else make their writing even better.

Selecting a Piece of Writing from a Previous Class and Allowing a Student to Revise and Edit the Piece on the Overhead

Let them talk through each step just as you have modeled for them.

Partnering Your Students and Letting Them Edit Each Other's Writing

After a mini-lesson on revising and editing, pair your students and let them edit each other's writing. If you partner students with similar writing abilities, they can appreciate and help each other. This is not something that all students can do, so sometimes you will find that a small group needs extra help. You can give them that extra help by gathering them around you and leading them in doing the editing of a piece.

Using Proofreader's Marks

If you want to teach the proofreader's marks, give the students a list of the marks and do a lesson on using them when editing. (See page 156 for a reproducible list of proofreader's marks.)

Mini-Lesson Focus: Capital Letters for Titles, Specific People, Events, and Places (Conventions)

By the time they reach the upper grades, students not only know that sentences begin with capital letters but should know that titles and proper nouns (specific people, events, and places) also begin with capital letters. This mini-lesson will remind students that they are accountable for the correct use of capital letters when they write. Talk about what you will write about and how you are going to focus on all of the ways to use capital letters in today's mini-lesson.

The teacher says:

"Today, I am going to write about some books that many students your age like to read. The books were so popular that they were made into movies. I have read two of the books, so I will tell you what I know about Harry Potter. As I write, I will remember to use capital letters when needed."

Wild about Harry Potter ("Titles need capital letters.")

Harry Potter and the Sorcerer's Stone ("Names or titles of books need capital letters.") was the first in a series of books about magic written by J.K. Rowling. ("People's names need capital letters. Sentences begin with capital letters.") Grown-ups and children alike were wildly enthusiastic about the book. ("Sentences begin with capital letters.") The second book, Harry Potter and the Chamber of Secrets ("another book title and more capital letters"), followed close behind. ("Sentences begin with capital letters.") She followed these with two more popular books ("two more book titles and more capital letters") Harry Potter and the Prisoner of Azkaban and Harry Potter and the Goblet of Fire.

For the next paragraph, the teacher may want to ask the students what she needs to do and why.

("What do I begin my sentence with? Why?") The books were all about Harry Potter. ("What do names need?") Harry ("What do names need?") goes to a school for wizards. At Hogwarts, ("What do names of places need?") Harry ("What do names need?") meets Ron ("What do names need?") and super-brainy Hermione. ("Another name—what does it need? How do I begin the next sentence?") There are many interesting teachers of magic including the great wizard, Dumbledore. ("Another name—what does it need?")

Add to the Writer's Checklist

5. I have used capital letters for titles, specific people, events, and places.

(Remind students that when they write they have to remember that proper nouns—names of people, places, and events—always begin with capital letters.)

Other Ideas for Capital Letters for Titles, Specific People, Events, and Places

Writing without Using Capital Letters, then Letting Students Edit Your Writing

my favorite authors

some of my favorite authors are katherine patterson, beverly cleary, dave pilkey, and gail gibbons. I also like books of poetry by shel silverstein.

who are your favorite authors?

Writing about What You Are Studying in Social Studies, Focusing on Capital Letters

In North Carolina, there are many places to visit. Some of the best known are the Outer Banks, Wilmington, Asheville, and Grandfather Mountain.

Writing about What You Are Studying in Social Studies, without Using Capital Letters, then Letting a Student or the Class Edit Your Writing

canada

canada has many provinces and also some territories. the provinces are british columbia, alberta, manitoba, saskatchewan, ontario, quebec, new brunswick, newfoundland and labrador, nova scotia, and prince edward island. The territories are the yukon, northwest, and the newest territory, nunavut.

Using a Capital Letter for the Pronoun "I"

If, after looking at your students' writing, you notice that some of them are still not capitalizing the pronoun "I," they may need a mini-lesson on this. Use a student's paper or write something and have students tell you what you did wrong. Often the offending students will realize why you have done this ("Because we do it!").

New York City

i like to go to New York City. When i am there, my favorite place to shop is Macy's. i always go to Little Italy to eat pasta. i go to musicals even though i think the tickets are very expensive; it is worth it.

Most of the Year—Continuing to Write

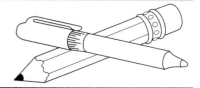

Mini-Lessons for Most of the Year

The most-of-the year mini-lessons assume that students will be spending some time in self-selected writing on topics of their own choosing and some time on focused writing on topics and genres chosen by the teacher. More items are added to the Writer's Checklist and students learn how to take a piece through the publishing process. Lessons are included to teach students how to write letters, book reviews, poetry, a biography, an informational article and a "How-to" piece. Lessons are also included on writing to a prompt. These lessons can be adapted to help you prepare for whatever kinds of writing tasks are required by your curriculum or your mandated writing assessments.

Mini-Lessons in this Section

Paragraphing in Stories and Informational Text

Reasons for Paragraphs and Indenting

Focused Writing: Memoir (7 mini-lessons)

> Choosing an Event, Narrowing the Focus
> Telling the Story in First Person
> Writing a Strong Lead
> An Emotional Hook, Sharing Your Feelings
> Using Transitions
> Fact or Fiction?
> Titles

Writing a Letter

Writing a Book Review or Movie Review

Writing Poetry

Publishing Procedures

Grammar—Adjectives and Descriptive Words

Grammar—Using Strong Verbs

Grammar—Nouns and Pronouns

Transitions in Writing

Modeling Revision Using a Think-Aloud

Focused Writing: Writing to a Prompt (9 mini-lessons)

> Generating a List of Suggestions for Writing to a Prompt
> Turning the Prompt Question into a Sentence
> How to Begin Writing to a Prompt

Mini-Lesson Focus: Paragraphing in Stories and Informational Text (Craft/Conventions)

Students in the upper grades need to understand paragraphs. A paragraph includes a group of sentences that are organized around a main idea. Every detail should support the main idea. It is important to teach students to plan before they begin to write, especially in content-area writing. A paragraph usually begins with a topic sentence that tells the reader what the paragraph is about. The paragraph usually contains enough sentences to give the reader all of the information needed to understand the topic of the paragraph. A closing sentence often "sums it up." Of course, not all paragraphs follow this structure, but many writers find this format useful when writing. You need to talk about the many kinds of paragraphs, and this is a good place to start.

The teacher says:

"Today I am going to write a paragraph about my visit to the White House. I could tell you many things, but I will focus on what I saw and the facts I learned while I was there. I may use a web to organize what I want to write about."

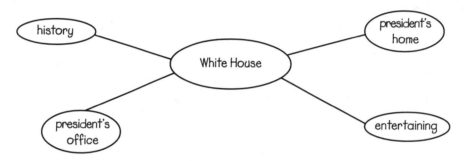

The teacher uses the web and talks as she writes:

> The White House is the home of the president of the United States. It is located in the nation's capital, Washington, D.C. There are 132 rooms in the White House today, but it was not always that big. It took George Washington eight years to build the first six rooms, and he never lived there. The White House did not have a bathroom when John Adams moved in. He was the first president to live in the White House. Today, it is both the home and office of the president. The president and his family live on the second floor. The president's office is called the oval office, and it is in a separate section of the White House with the other offices. The White House has many elegant rooms where the president and his wife entertain royalty and important people from all over the world. The White House is an important building.

Because her students write paragraphs quite well, the teacher may want to write four paragraphs using her web, taking four days and also modeling "adding on." She writes one paragraph on the history of the White House, one on where the president and first family live, another on the oval office, and a final paragraph on how the president and first lady entertain in the White House.

Other Ideas for Paragraphing in Stories and Informational Text

Writing Descriptive Paragraphs

A descriptive paragraph describes a person, place, or thing. Writers use the five senses and figurative language—including personification, onomatopoeia, and comparisons—when writing descriptive paragraphs. They do this so that the reader will feel like they are really there.

During your teacher read-aloud, read some descriptive paragraphs and talk about them. One of the best descriptions can be found in E.B. White's *Charlotte's Web* (HarperTrophy, 1999) as he describes the barn. Katherine Patterson also writes wonderful descriptions; in her book *Bridge to Terabithia* (HarperTrophy, 1987), you feel like you are running across the field with Leslie. One of the best ways to teach descriptive writing is to show the class how you write descriptions.

> The bright, beautiful morning sun was rising above the clean, blue lake. The day was already hot, and steam was already rising from the water. The . . . .

Writing Persuasive Paragraphs

In a persuasive paragraph, a view is stated, and the writer tries to sway the readers to her point of view. Many students find persuasive paragraphs easy to write if they have opinions on the subjects. They can tell you their favorite restaurants, movies, or books and why; then they go into detail on their reasons.

> I like spring because the days get longer and everything is in bloom. I . . . .

Writing Narrative Paragraphs

In a narrative paragraph, students write the events to tell a story. Students use structures such as beginning, middle, and end when writing a story. To model these narrative paragraphs, take a day to model writing the beginning, a day to model writing the middle, and a day to model writing the end of a story. (You might need another day to revise and edit!)

Writing Expository Paragraphs

In expository paragraphs, the writer provides information by using sequence, comparison, cause and effect, and other text structures. The piece may explain how to do something or give directions. When you write about science, social studies, or health topics, you will need to teach students to organize the material, and then use these types of paragraphs to write. In social studies you may compare two cities, states, or periods in history. When writing about a science experiment, you need to tell what you did first, what happened next, and finally what the results were.

> The experiment started with gathering the needed materials. First, we . . . .

Using Punctuation in Paragraphs

Punctuation marks signal grammatical boundaries and express meaning. Quotation marks are used most often to indicate what someone is saying. As you write narrative paragraphs, talk about the quotations marks and paragraph changes needed for writing conversations, if they are wanted and needed in writing narrative paragraphs. Commas are often needed when writing descriptions to separate things in a series.

> She pulled on her big, heavy, wooly, brown sweater. She was warmer but . . . .

Mini-Lesson Focus: Reasons for Paragraphs and Indenting (Conventions)

Students need real reasons to start new paragraphs. When writing expository text, it is fine to stick to the "rule" you so often hear: start a new paragraph when you talk about a new topic/subject or change ideas. However, writing narrative pieces, which many students do most of the time, calls for more than this one rule. There are two rules to avoid: a paragraph has a certain number of sentences and a paragraph can never be one sentence long. Both of these rules can be proven wrong by looking at nearly any book a student has read. Students can learn the ways to paragraph, as subjective as it is. Teach this lesson by examining an excerpt of text your students are familiar with. Choose the excerpt carefully. You will need a model that provides clear examples of differing reasons for new paragraphs. A good example we might suggest is on pages 42 and 43 of *Number the Stars* by Lois Lowry (Houghton Mifflin Co., 1989).

The teacher says:

"Today, we want to talk about the reasons we start a new paragraph. I can tell from your writing that you already know to indent when you begin a new paragraph. The hard part is trying to decide when to start a new one.

"I've brought an excerpt from the story we are reading aloud right now, and I want you to spend some time looking at it. Let's read through the paragraphs on this overhead and think about why the author started each new paragraph."

The teacher looks at the excerpt she has chosen for her students and shares the examples with them. (If this is the first introduction to paragraphing, don't ask for reasons why the new paragraphs were started. Give them the reasons for starting a new paragraph and see which reasons were used in the example you've provided.)

"Let me show you the reasons we start new paragraphs. I am going to make a list on this chart, and you are going to copy the list down. Then, I will make copies of this excerpt for you, and you can tape the excerpt into your writing handbooks as an example."

Reasons for New Paragraphs in Stories

1. Setting changes (In the kitchen . . . . , Back at the farm . . . . , etc.)
2. Time changes (The next morning. At 10:00 p.m.)
3. Topic or idea changes
4. *A new person is talking during the dialogue

*Only include this on the list if you've had a discussion about paragraphing dialogue.

"As you look over this list, which type of paragraph changes do you think we saw in our example? Let's mark them."

Today, as I begin to write a story, I will indent my paragraphs just as you will when . . . .

Add to the Writer's Checklist:

6. I have new paragraphs in the right places, and they are indented.

Other Ideas for Paragraphs and Indenting

Having Students Look for Examples

Ask students to bring their self-selected books to the mini-lesson. Review the list of different types of paragraph changes and have students look through their own stories for examples of each type. Before you ask them to look, provide a few examples from different texts you've used as read-alouds. Let the students share a few examples as a class, then turn to a neighbor and share one example they found.

Working Together to Make Paragraphing Decisions

Find an excerpt from another book you've read aloud. Retype the excerpt from the text including no paragraphs. Type it as one big block of text. Begin by demonstrating one of the reasons we use paragraphs—to give readers a break. When we look at that one big block of text, it is intimidating. No one wants to read it.

Now, read through it with your students to make decisions about where to make the paragraph breaks. Check yourselves against the real text. You may not make exactly the same decisions about the paragraphs. That is okay if your students can give a reason for why the paragraph should occur.

Paragraphing Made Easier

(This idea came from a second-grade classroom—Thanks, Joyce Chittum!—and has been used in a third-grade classroom.) If these other lessons seem too advanced to begin with, try this easier approach to paragraphing. The piece below really needs to be two paragraphs but is written as one. Share it with students and ask them to help you make it better. It is really about two different things: the author's job and the traveling she does. One suggestion is to cut the piece apart sentence by sentence and put it back together in a better order, making it two paragraphs.

> Sometimes when I work, I have to travel out of town. My job is to work with teachers. I will be in Colorado all of next week. Sometimes I spend time doing lessons with students in classrooms. On Tuesday and Wednesday, I will be in Rifle, CO, and on Thursday and Friday, I will be in Colorado Springs. The teachers are my students. Other times, I spend time visiting with teachers. I will fly to Colorado on Monday. Being gone from home is hard, but I love my job!

How you rearrange your two paragraphs is up to the students. They may not put them in the order you thought they should be in, however, if students give reasons, the paragraphs may work fine more than one way. If your students need this beginning step, try it before the other suggested lessons.

Focused Writing: Memoir (Craft—7 Mini-Lessons)

"Memoir is how writers look for the past and make sense of it. We figure out who we are, who we have become, and what it means to us and to the lives of others: a memoir puts the events of a life in perspective for the writer and those who read it. It is a way to validate to others the events of our lives—our choices, perspectives, decisions, responses." (Atwell, 1998)

After reading Nancie Atwell's definition of a memoir, it is easy to understand that a memoir calls a student to move beyond what we, in education, have often referred to as the personal narrative. A memoir makes a difference. It matters. For those reasons, we need to use the criteria that define a memoir to shape the mini-lessons necessary to model the genre to our students. Begin with the end in mind, as we will suggest for other focused writing. Think about what you want the memoir to contain, what you want it to do for the writer, and what you want it to do for the reader.

Be sure to give prior consideration to an event in your own life that would be a good example to use. You will be writing a memoir in front of your students to model the process. The mini-lessons you conduct will allow you to think aloud in front of your students as a writer. There may also be times you will need to do some of the writing in preparation for the next day's mini-lesson.

Memoir Mini-Lessons

Day 1: Choosing an Event, Narrowing the Focus

Day 2: Telling the Story in First Person

Day 3: Writing a Strong Lead

Day 4: An Emotional Hook, Sharing your Feelings

Day 5: Using Transitions

Day 6: Fact or Fiction?

Day 7: Titles

This genre is a less-threatening experience for writers at the beginning of the year. Most of your students will be accustomed to writing about personal experiences. Your mini-lessons will be used to guide students' choices to events that had personal significance. The "memory" will be retold through the author's perspective.

As with the other focused genres in this book, there are specific examples included with most of the mini-lessons. The examples are there as models for the teacher. You will be a more effective model for your students if you find your own topics to write about.

The topic chosen for these memoir mini-lessons didn't happen to you. Hopefully, however, by reading the examples provided, it will provide insight for the process used. As uncomfortable as it might feel, it will be important for you to write about your own significant memory. The best teachers of writing are writers.

Time Frame

In this section, there are seven mini-lessons for how you might teach a memoir. It is assumed that your students will work for two to three weeks on their own memoirs. Below is a chart to represent the use of time.

	Mini-Lesson	Students	Teacher
Week 1	Lessons 1-5	Begin to get information from mini-lessons and brainstorm possible topics; work through steps as guided in the mini-lessons.	Use the mini-lessons to write your own memoir; use conferencing time to ensure each student has a narrow focus.
Week 2	Lessons 6-7 Follow up with any topics students still need help with.	Work on memoir.	Mini-lessons focus on the genre and any topics students still need assistance with; conference to assist in the necessary stages of writing.
Week 3	Give short mini-lessons on necessary topics but allow more time for conferences.	Work on memoir. Memoir is due.	Conferences should be publishing conferences. You will want short mini-lessons to allow more time to confer.

You will decide if your students need more time to finish this genre. Don't let the genre take more than three to four weeks. Remember how important it is to reserve time for writing on topics of choice.

This genre, along with several other focused genres, requires you to spend time reading examples of the genre prior to its teaching. There is a list of professional resources at the end of the mini-lessons (page 150). Among those resources you will find titles of picture-book memoirs and chapter-book memoirs. Find the resources you will need to use as models for your students.

Mini-Lesson Focus: Choosing an Event, Narrowing the Focus (Craft)

Day 1

As we've already demonstrated in the mini-lessons, it is important for writers to understand that the best writing is very narrowly focused. This is especially true of a memoir. There is significance in the event chosen for a memoir. Model for your students how to choose a topic that made an impact and is also narrow in scope.

The teacher says:

"We've read some examples of the genre we call memoir over the past couple of weeks. Today, we will begin our study and exploration of that particular genre. Each of you will be writing a memoir. To do that, the first step is choosing your topic. We've already spent several days this year learning how to look for and list topics. I shared my own writing list with you more than once. But, if I think back to my writing list, my ideas on that list aren't all topics that would work to write a memoir. One of the things that I know about a memoir is that it needs to be a memory that is significant to me. The memory had an impact on my life; I will be the main character. If you remember some of the things I've already written or talked about, you know that I am not the main character. For example, when Merrill Kaye was chased by the Canada geese, I was there, and I certainly remember that day. However, it was not something that changed me.

"So, as I thought of a memory that would work well for a memoir, I thought about something that is not even on my writing list. In fact, it happened when I was in the eighth grade, and I still remember it so clearly. That is one way for me to know it had an impact . . . it is impossible to forget. I was hit by a car in the eighth grade in front of most of the members of my eighth-grade class . . . at least it seemed that way.

"I think this will work pretty well because it is one event, and it is already narrow in focus. Remember when we talked about narrowing the topic a few days ago? It will be really important for you to find a narrow topic. In other words, if you went on a great vacation this summer and you have some significant memories of that, that topic would be too broad. But, you could think to yourself, what is the one thing I did on my vacation that had an impact? Maybe you saw the ocean for the first time, that could be a significant memory. Sometimes the significant memories we have are unhappy ones. A memoir I plan to write someday is about the day my mom died. I know that will be an unhappy story to tell, but it is very specific and narrow in focus.

"As you begin to think of topics that will work for your memoirs, remember the things we've talked about today. The memory should be very clear, it should be significant or make a difference, and it should be narrow in focus.

"Take some time now to look over your writing lists or to think of other ideas that would work well for memoirs."

The teacher creates a chart with the criteria for the topic. Her students are expected to take notes on what makes a memoir a memoir, and these criteria will help with the definition.

Memoirs

1. The memory is very clear.
2. The memory is significant or makes a difference.
3. The memory is narrow in focus.

Mini-Lesson Focus: Telling the Story in First Person (Craft)

Day 2

A memoir makes a difference in the life of the author, therefore, the author tells it as her story. Not only is the author the main character, but the story is told in first person—from the author's perspective. It will be easiest to model this style by reading other examples of memoirs written just that way. There are several student-written memoirs in Nancie Atwell's *In The Middle* (Heinemann, 1987). Reading these examples, along with published books, will help children "see" the genre of memoir.

The teacher says:

"How many of you know what it means to tell a story in first person? Have you noticed that the memoirs we've been reading have been told that way? Think about *When I Was Young In the Mountains* by Cynthia Rylant (E. P. Dutton, 1993). Even the title uses the word 'I.' A memoir is your story, so you will tell it using the first-person reference: I.

"I know that I could call some of my friends from middle school and ask them about the day I got hit by a car. I've heard the stories from many of them, lots of different times. Their stories are different from mine because we all experienced it in different ways.

"As I write my memoir, I will tell my version and my perception of the memory of being hit by a car. You will tell your memory from your perspective just as all the authors did in the examples we've listened to.

"Spend a little more time today thinking about a topic or brainstorming the details you will include as you tell your memory to an audience. Think back to the examples you've heard."

Memoirs

1. The memory is very clear.
2. The memory is significant or makes a difference.
3. The memory is narrow in focus.
4. The memory is told in first person.

As you begin to create this list of criteria, you begin to define your expectations. This should help with the creation of a scoring guide or should match a scoring guide you've already developed. A logical next step would be to present the scoring guide to your students during the next mini-lesson. We are not going to offer a scoring guide in this book, as it needs to be developed to meet the needs of the instruction going on in each classroom/district. However, if you have a scoring guide, use your next mini-lesson to go over the guide with your class. Then, use the remaining mini-lessons to demonstrate the information contained in the scoring guide.

If you do not have a scoring guide for this genre, you should begin collaboration to develop one. A scoring guide acts as a target for the writer. The guide should be developed to be shared with the students. A scoring guide developed only for the teacher does not assist students in finding ways to better their writing.

Looking Ahead

For tomorrow's mini-lesson write two or three different leads for your own memoir. You can use different starting points or write a "good" one and a "bad" one.

Mini-Lesson Focus: Writing a Strong Lead (Craft)

Day 3

Drawing the reader in is the object of the lead. Students will have mini-lessons on strong leads during choice writing as well as focused writing. It is an issue authors must deal with for each piece of writing. If you've already done other mini-lessons on writing strong leads, draw on the previously presented information. If not, do some research. Find some strong leads written specifically as parts of memoirs. Read them aloud to your students. Work with them to either develop some categories or characteristics of leads that appeal to them.

The teacher says:

"Today, we need to begin thinking about how to start our memoirs. We've talked about strong leads before; at least, we've read some in the books I've read aloud to you this year and in the samples of memoirs we've been reading recently. I know I want the readers of my memoir to be drawn in right away. I have to think of a way to pique their interest right from the beginning.

"I've tried a couple of leads for my story, and I want you to help me decide which one to use. There are different ways to organize the telling of a story. My first lead starts in the middle of the action. Sometimes, I think it is exciting to read stories that start right in the middle of an exciting part. Then, I will have to back up and give some details of what happened before the climax. Listen to this . . . ."

> I couldn't believe I was having this dream again. I turned my head to the side expecting to wake up in my bed. Instead, I discovered I was lying in the middle of Business Loop 44 with the eighth grade football team and the middle school cheerleaders looking on. No way . . . I had been hit by a car!

"That is one way I am thinking of starting my story. Do you think that would draw the readers in? I hoped that by telling right away that I had been hit by a car, the reader would want to know how it happened and why all of the other kids were right there watching. Listen to this . . . ."

> I can remember lots of things about being in middle school. Some things I remember better than others. However, there was a certain day in September of my eighth grade year that many people won't forget. I can still see it in my mind, just like it was yesterday . . . .

"Now, this time, I was trying to lead the reader in without giving away the big event. Do you think you would want to keep reading to find out what it is I remember so clearly? I think either lead would work for my memoir. But, the one I choose will change the order I tell the story. Make sure you look at your lead to see how your story will need to be told.

"Today, I want you to try some different leads for your memoir. You might want to write three or four to try different techniques. You might just write one, then reread and fine tune what you want to say. Your lead may determine the order you tell your memory, just like mine did. If that is the case, you might also do some prewriting to decide that order."

Looking Ahead

In tomorrow's lesson, you will be modeling how to show the reader what the author is feeling and the emotions that are involved. You will want to think of one or two places in your own memory to share. The important thing is to show the reader, not just tell the reader. Show; don't tell!

Mini-Lesson Focus: An Emotional Hook, Sharing Your Feelings (Craft)

Day 4

Part of a memoir is to let the audience know why this memory is significant, why it matters. Perception of the event should include feelings and emotions. More than likely, the event wouldn't be significant to the author if no emotions were involved. The hardest part will be for students to show these feelings through actions, dialogue, thoughts, etc. More than likely, young writers will want to tell how they were feeling. Showing is always better than telling. Use emotional excerpts from your own memoir to model how readers can "see" and "feel" the way the author feels.

The teacher says:

"Yesterday, we began working on our leads. We know the importance of each piece of writing, including a way to draw the reader in. Let's add that to the list of things we know about a memoir. Today, we're adding one more idea to our list about memoirs. As we chose our topics, we chose things that were significant or made a difference.

"Those types of memories are clearly tied to your emotions or feelings. It will be an important part of your memoir to show those feelings to the reader. It may seem easier to tell the reader, but showing makes a better story. Sometimes, we want readers to have to figure a few things out about our stories. I've written about some of the emotions I went through when I was hit by a car. Listen to it both ways and decide which one you would rather read. Did I show you how I felt? Or, did I tell you how I felt?"

> Okay, here I am lying in the middle of the road in front of the football team, not to mention, I'm wearing my cheerleading uniform. Tomorrow . . . at school . . . oh, no! I know I looked both ways before I crossed the street. Where in the world did this car come from?

> I was so embarrassed. I couldn't believe I had been hit by a car in front of all of those people. I was sure they were laughing at me. I really didn't want to see them at school tomorrow.

"Can you see how I told my feelings in one paragraph, and I tried to show how I was feeling in the other? You can probably imagine that I was embarrassed without my telling you. I think you can relate to how it must have felt to have something like this happen to you in front of lots of other people. As you write your memoirs, you'll want your readers to feel what you felt and see what you saw. Use the language of the story to show them."

Memoirs

1. The memory is very clear
2. The memory is significant or makes a difference
3. The memory is narrow in focus
4. The memory is told in first person
5. A strong lead draws the reader in
6. Show the reader your emotions/feelings

Mini-Lesson Focus: Using Transitions (Craft)

Day 5

Transitions assist the reader. They can establish time, place, order, and even breaks. Young writers often use only time order words, and usually, ineffectively. There are many transitions other than: next, then, before, etc. Again, an effective way to heighten the awareness of the writer, is to expose them to transitions in writing. Even in a simple text, transitions assist the reader. For this mini-lesson, choose a book your students have heard. Use the book to determine which transitions were used and how they helped.

The teacher says:

"The best writing includes transitions. Does anyone know what a transition is? Could you give me an example of one? Why do you think we use transitions when writing?" (As you lead this discussion with your students, make sure they understand new paragraphs are often started with transitions, transitions can establish a change in setting, transitions help to organize the sequence of the story, and transitions—just like the beginnings of new paragraphs—can give the reader breaks.)

"Let's look at the book by Cynthia Rylant, *When I Was Young In The Mountains*. We've read that book a couple of times, and you know it is a short picture book, categorized as a memoir. This time, as we read it, listen for the transitions. I want to list some of the choices Cynthia Rylant made as she wrote her memory down.

"Cynthia Rylant used a repeating transition throughout her book, it was even her title. Most of us won't be able to use that technique. But, some of her other transitions could be used. Many of her transitions helped to establish a time frame or helped with the sequence. When she said 'on our way home' she was also establishing setting along with the timing.

"It will not be possible for you to choose your transitions now, without doing the writing itself. However, as you write, look to see if transitions could help your readers make more sense of the memory you are telling."

Transitions

When I was young in the mountains

Later, in the middle of the night,

Afterward

Sometimes

On our way home

There is another mini-lesson including many more transitions later in the book (page 70). You may decide that the idea of transitions is too much to deal with as you introduce the genre of memoir. If so, just skip this mini-lesson. As always, make the lesson fit the needs of your students.

Mini-Lesson Focus: Fact or Fiction? (Craft)

Day 6

Think of the stories your family has told and retold for generations. The stories themselves are factual. Each time they are retold, a bit of fiction may creep in. The conversations are embellished or exaggeration takes over. The same may be true of a memoir. When we tell stories from our own perspectives, we tell the facts as we've interpreted them. If we were to ask someone else to retell the same story, there would, no doubt, be a bit of a different "spin." Memoirs are told with the author's "spin." If the memory took place many years ago, more than likely exact conversations are not quotable, but they are remembered. The event really happened, that is crucial, but if the facts are a bit "fuzzy," it won't hurt a thing.

The teacher says:

"Are these memoirs we're writing fact or fiction? (Hopefully, the response will be fact.) Right, we are writing about factual events from our own lives. I told you the event I am writing about happened to me when I was in eighth grade. You know, that has been quite a while ago for me, in fact it was more than 20 years ago! Do you think I remember everything that was said that day? Do you think I remember what the police officer said to me when the ambulance was coming? Well, if I don't remember exactly what was said, how can I be sure I am writing facts?

"You see, in memoirs, we are writing about a memory the way we remember it ourselves. Will it be okay if I use dialogue between myself and Dr. Williams, even if I don't really remember what was said word for word? I bet there are stories you remember from an age when you were really too young to remember. Here is what I mean. My youngest, Lafe, "remembers" sliding down the stairs on his tummy when he was only about 2½. Now, when I asked him why he did such a thing, he told me 'that is just what little boys do.' I don't think Lafe really remembers doing that or saying that, but we've told the story so many times, he "remembers" it through us.

"While this memoir does need to be something you really remember, it will also have details that may, in actuality, be made up. Tell the story as you remember it. Make sure the reader knows why it made a difference or why it is significant to you and keep the focus narrow. That is what will make it a memoir."

In your examples of writing your own memoir, be sure to point out places where the fact and fiction are a bit blurry. Dialogue is usually a good place to start. Most of us don't remember word for word what was said 2 years ago, much less 20 years ago. Stick to telling a factual story but include the details that only **you** might remember.

Mini-Lesson Focus: Titles (Craft)

Day 7

This is the last mini-lesson for a reason. Too often kids want to write a title as the very first thing. Again, use examples of books you've read to lead a discussion on how different titles were chosen. Have students wait on writing or selecting titles until nearer the end of their writing.

The teachers says:

"I haven't given my memoir a title yet. Some of you have asked me what I will call my story. A title is a very important part of the story, and we give different titles for different reasons. Just the other day, my daughter started reading *Tuck Everlasting* by Natalie Babbit (Farrar, Straus, and Giroux, 1975), and after just a few pages she asked me if the book was *Tuck Everlasting*, why was is about the Fosters? I told her she would have to keep reading to find out. Titles can be like that, sometimes you have to read **most** of the book or story to find out why the title was chosen.

"Once, I read a book by John Grisham, called *The Rainmaker* (Island Books, 1996). I read the whole thing and still didn't know why it was called *The Rainmaker*. I was discussing the book with a friend, and he explained to me that a lawyer in a law firm who makes all of the money is often referred to as the rainmaker of the firm. Well, that wasn't explained in the book, so I didn't understand. But, people who know that term understood the title.

"Sometimes, a title names a certain character; sometimes, it is almost a summary or a statement about what happened. Choosing your title should come near the end or even as the last thing when you are writing. Take some time to really think about what your title could do for your story. I've tried to come up with a couple of different ones to see what you think."

> 1. It is Just Another Dream
> 2. Two Broken Legs, a Broken Arm, and a Concussion

"The first one you might understand. Remember in my lead, I said I thought I was having a dream when I first got hit by the car. Later in the story I explain that I had dreamed about being hit by a car not too long before it happened. So, I thought that title might work.

"The other title is explained more toward the end of my memoir. You see, that night I went to the football game after I finished at the doctor's office. I was really lucky, because I only had some scrapes and bruises, and I was pretty sore. But as always, in a small town, by the time I got to the game the rumor was that I had flipped over the car and I had many broken bones, head injuries—you get the picture. Most people were making it out to be much worse than it was. So, I thought the title might make people want to read the memoir because it sounds like a terrible accident. Then, they would read to find out the injuries didn't amount to much at all.

"I personally thought both of these titles were better than something like 'Being Hit By a Car.' What do you think? If you've already written your title, read it to yourself and decide if you think the title draws the reader in. Did you just state a brief summary of your story or did you spend some time deciding on a title that fits your story well? If you are not finished with your memoir yet, you can wait to make a decision about your title. Just remember the types of titles we talked about today when you are ready."

Ideas for Memoir at Different Grade Levels

It is only logical and even important that more than one grade level provide instruction on memoir. It is the type of writing your children will most often choose to do: personal experience that made a difference. Even if several grade levels in your building will be using these mini-lessons as the guide, there should not be a problem. Each teacher will take on a personal style in implementing the lesson. A school or district would benefit from a conversation to decide which grades will address which genres. Then, if memoir, for example, is taught at both fourth and fifth grades, a different emphasis can be decided. Below are some examples or suggestions for how that might work.

Third Grade

At this age, just stick with the basics of teaching the genre of memoir. Remember the most important criteria: a personal memory, significance, and told in first person. Using just the examples provided would be enough information at the basic level.

Fourth Grade

Strong leads make such a difference for any piece of text. It would be a great emphasis for this piece of writing at this age. If a strong lead is important, it will be necessary that you spend more than one day modeling and discussing ways to write a strong lead.

Then, if using a scoring guide, that element would be addressed clearly on the guide. Students would work together to listen to each other's leads and make good decisions about how to draw the reader in.

Fifth Grade

If your fifth graders have been given instruction for a year or more on how to write a memior, much of your instruction will be approached as review. In other words, instead of making a list of criteria with you determining what should appear, it would be much more asking the students to remember what they know about this genre.

Their information or memory may not be as accurate or detailed as you would like. Adapt your instruction accordingly. If in fourth grade, your students were working on strong leads as an emphasis, fifth grade could choose to look at endings. How does the student wrap it up? Or, you might choose descriptive/figurative language. Either of these elements will also enhance the final product of a memoir.

Having the criteria remain constant throughout the grades should add to knowledge of the genre. Students will see the consistency and know what a memoir is at every age. The instructional focus can make the experience a bit different for the students at multiple grade levels.

Mini-Lesson Focus: Writing a Letter (Craft/Procedures)

For older students, this lesson will most likely be a review. Writing letters is a task and genre that is user friendly for young students. When deciding to do this lesson, and introduce this genre, it will be most successful if there is a need or a reason for your students to be writing a letter. If your class is gathering information for a study of some kind and your students need to write to someone to ask for the information, that is the time to teach them how to write a letter. If you have class pen pals and you expect your students to use a letter format, do this mini-lesson. In other words, don't do the mini-lesson, then insist that your students come up with reasons for writing letters.

The teachers says:

"Today, we're going to review what a letter looks like on the page. I know most of you will have no trouble at all with this. However, if you really need to write a letter to someone, it is important to know what should be included in that letter. We've spent a lot of time this year talking about what readers expect when they look at certain things. Letters are no different. So, who can remind me of the five parts of a friendly letter?

"Right—heading, greeting, body, closing, signature. Each of those parts also needs to be in a certain location. A letter, just like a poem, looks a certain way on the page. I'm going to show you where those parts belong."

October 31, 2002

Dear Aunt Margie and Jean,

It was so good to see you all on your last visit. Even though you stay for several weeks, the time goes too quickly, and we're always sad when it is time for you to head back to Washington.

The students are already asking when we will see you again. I know we need to make a trip out there next time. It is such beautiful country. We'll be in touch soon.

Love,

Amanda

"If you were to just glance at this paper, without even reading the words, wouldn't you know you were about to read a letter? It looks like a letter, and it has all the parts of a letter. In a friendly letter, the heading (which is the date) closing, and signature, are lined up on the paper. The greeting is always lined up with the left side of the paper, and the body is indented. When you write a letter, your reader will expect to see those things. Any questions?"

Other Ideas for Writing a Letter

Writing a Business Letter

For this lesson, students should be able to make a connection to the friendly letter. However, a business letter has more components and is more formal. Students need to understand the need for formality, so that if they are truly in need of sending a business letter, they will be taken seriously.

Heading:	address of the person sending the letter
	starts in the middle of the top line of the page
Inside address:	includes the name of the recipient
	full address
	aligned with the left margin
Greeting:	aligned with the left margin
	ends with a colon, not a comma
Body:	is indented
	last paragraph needs to thank the person for his time
Closing:	aligned with the heading included at the top
	should be an appropriate choice such as, sincerely
Signature:	cursive signature with sender's name typed or handwritten underneath

Writing a Thank-You Note

All of the genres included in these lessons are lifelong genres. Students should know how to send an appropriate letter or thank-you note. The best mini-lesson is to write in front of the students. Write a note you need to send in front of your students. Write it on the overhead or on chart paper, then include showing them an appropriate type of paper to use for the thank-you note. Let students see that thank-you notes are a part of real life.

Writing an Invitation

This lesson can be taught when your class is preparing to invite parents or other students to view their writing, or for any other reason. Again, it is easiest for students to learn when they see a real need. Bring in sample invitations you've sent or received. Even if "fluff" is included, let students see what information is always included.

Writing a Sympathy Note

This is a difficult lesson to teach and a difficult one to learn. If your class is unfortunate enough to have lost someone close, or perhaps a student lost a close relative, it is a time to teach students what to say. Sympathy notes are difficult for adults to write. Learning what is appropriate and how to express yourself in a personal way is another lifelong lesson. Again, write in front of your students. You may choose to do this lesson when you need to write a note outside of class. Then, if your students really do need this genre, it won't be so hard to talk about.

Add to Writer's Handbook: Examples of punctuation and format for letters.

Mini-Lesson Focus: Writing a Book Review or Movie Review (Craft)

Once again, the emphasis of this mini-lesson is to teach students about genres that exist in real life, not just in schools. A book report is a school genre, and an ineffective one at that. However, book reviews can be found in major newspapers, magazines, and professional journals. It is a real-life genre read by many different types of people. A movie review is similar. These real-life genres may appeal to a population of your students that are not "turned on" by stories. Our job is to expose children to all types of writing. For those students who spend lots of time reading books, a book review is a natural connection for writing. Similarly, those who watch lots of movies may be your best movie reviewers.

The teacher says:

"Today, I brought in some reviews that I want us to think about. Have any of you ever noticed book reviews in magazines? Sometimes, you will also see movie reviews. Today, we are going to look at a lot of examples. I found some in *People*, *Time*, and *Newsweek*. I even brought in some reviews written by students that are published in a journal called *Voices from the Middle*.

"Many of you may have written book reports in other classrooms. That experience may help you a little as we talk about writing a book review. Let's read one together, and then I want you to tell me why you think the review was written."

(Read several examples with students and help them generate a list of characteristics they see in the reviews. By bringing in samples from different places, they will see the similarities and differences. If you have access to a major newspaper, most of them also carry book reviews. Create a file of examples that your students can refer to. The student-written examples from *Voices from the Middle* will be essential. Students need to see the quality of other students' writing.)

The teacher reads a book review, talks about it with the students, and writes:

In this book review, the writer:

- told about the topic of the book

- tave some details in the story

- did not tell the conclusion

- told about the magic (humor, sadness)

- told how he liked the book

- told about what he thought was missing

Two excellent resources for writing book reviews are: *Teaching Reading in Middle School* by Laura Robb (Scholastic, 2000) and *In the Middle: New Understandings About Writing, Reading and Learning* by Nancie Atwell (Heinemann, 1998). Both authors offer a copy of the list of requirements and criteria that they expect their students to include. By introducing this genre to students, you get beyond the bland summary so often written in a book report. The idea behind a review is to encourage or discourage other readers. This is a real-life reading behavior. Readers tell other readers about which books to read and which books to avoid.

Other Ideas for Writing a Book Review or Movie Review

Writing a Movie Review

Use the same process used for the book review. It is important to have examples of this genre for students to read. Bring in copies of movie reviews from magazines and newspapers. Again, write a list of what the reviewer wrote about as seen in the example. (Using the movie review titled, "The Eminem Story," in *Newsweek*, November 11, 2002, by David Ansen about the movie, *8 Mile*.)

This movie reviewer:

- writes about the story in this movie

- tells us about the life of Eminem (Marshall Mathers)

- compares Eminem's life to the rapper in the movie named Rabbit

- credits the director with "keeping it real"

- writes that the movie has an exhilarating climax but does not tell it

- likes the performances of the two actresses who play Rabbit's mother (Kim Basinger) and girlfriend (Brittany Murphy)

- says it is too early to call Eminem a Hollywood giant, but the promise is there

Watching a Movie Together as a Class, then Writing a Review Together as a Class

If the class has viewed a movie together at school, model the process by writing a review together for your mini-lesson.

Reading a Book, Watching the Movie, then Writing a Review

After reading a book together as a class, watch the movie. Summarize the book and compare it to the movie. Did the movie stay true to the book? Which did the class like best? Why?

Writing a Music Review

Allow your students to adapt the review format and write a review of a favorite CD. Again, some magazines will have music reviews to show as examples. This is a cultural connection for your students. It is a way to bring in the music they feel connected to and review it for an audience of their peers.

Mini-Lesson Focus: Writing Poetry (Craft/Procedures)

This lesson is used for the purpose of showing students how an alternate genre can provide a break from their writing. If you are working on writing poetry as a focus, however, this lesson could be incorporated into the instruction as well.

Students, as well as adults, can work on pieces for a long time and feel they just need to put them away for a while—even a day or more. If that is the case, sometimes poetry can be a nice genre to fall back on. The type of poetry shown below has no real name (though we will call it a "list" poem). It seems to be an easy type of poetry for students to try and moves them away from feeling they must rhyme when writing poems.

The teacher says:

"You know I've been working on a story for a while now, and today I don't really feel like going back to it. Have you ever had that happen? I mean, I know I want to finish the story, I just think I want to take a break today. Sometimes when I take a break, I like to try writing a poem. It's the kind of poem that doesn't have to rhyme, which makes it much easier to write. I call it a "list" poem because I use the poem to make a list of things associated with one topic. It is a list of my thoughts or connections to the topic or title. I want to write one for you today, and we might even write one together tomorrow or another day.

> Mizzou Football
> Black and gold
> Tailgating
> Marching Mizzou
> The Missouri Waltz
> Seeing friends and family
> Faurot Field
> M-I-Z-Z-O-U
> Winning some, losing some
> Going for 17 years
> All the yummy food
> "Here come the Tigers!"
> Memorial Stadium

"As I was thinking about what I might write today, I thought it might be fun to write about going to the University of Missouri Tigers' football games. I associate that with the fall, and I've been going for so long, I can't imagine not going. So, I think I will try it out."

> Mizzou Football
> Tailgating
> Seeing friends and family
> All the yummy food
> Black and gold
> Faurot Field in Memorial Stadium
> "Here come the Tigers!"
> Marching Mizzou
> "Hey, Hey Baby"
> M-I-Z-Z-O-U
> Winning some, losing some
> Always a faithful fan
> Going for 17 years
> Mizzou football

"Now, I've just made a list of the things I think of. I want to spend some time deciding how I want it to sound. Poetry has to have rhythm, and I need to think about how I could make this one better. I will make some changes to get the poem in the form I want. I also end the poem by using the same line as I put in the title, so I will say "Mizzou Football" again at the end.

"If some of you would like to try a list poem today, that would be fine. Some of you may be in the middle of something and not want to take a break from it. Just remember how to write a poem like this."

(Either at sharing time, at the end of the writing block, or the next day during your mini-lesson, share with students your finished poem. Think aloud for them about the decisions you made to combine some lines, add some lines, and why you rearranged them. Editing and revising marks will be on the original list you made, and you can show that page and compare it with the finished product.)

Other Ideas for Writing Poetry

Writing Cinquains

Writing a cinquain is a favorite of teachers and students. A cinquain consists of five unrhymed lines that are usually made up of two, four, six, eight, and two syllables. A simplified variation that is made up of one word, two words, three words, four words, and one word is easier and may be where some classes need to start. Read a cinquain; then, read the directions and discuss what has to be written and why. Then, it is your students' turn to write.

> City
> New York
> Busy, crowded, noisy
> Shopping, watching, eating, hurrying
> Fun!

Writing Acrostic Poems

An easy lesson for early in the year is to let the students use their names. Acrostic poems can be made from book characters, holidays, and social studies characters or places.

> Cheerful
> Happy
> Athletic
> Daring

Discussing Poets and Poetry

Make copies of several poems by one poet (Shel Silverstein, Myra Cohn Livingston, E. E. Cummings, etc.) for the students (or write them on an overhead transparency). You could also use poems by several authors that address one topic. Read the poems to the class. The copies are important, so that your students see what the poetry you are reading looks like. Try writing poetry in a similar style or topic for your students or with your students in this mini-lesson. Put the poetry in your files for them to refer to throughout the year. Add poetry to your writing list.

Mini-Lesson Focus: Publishing Procedures (Procedures)

By now, your students are writing, and they are getting quite good. They have learned how to revise, and self-edit, and many are doing so without your help. Students in all grade levels need to know that not everything is published, therefore they do not need to revise and edit everything they write. A quick edit is a good daily habit, to make sure that their first drafts say what they wanted them to say. But, many students need a reason to take some of their writing through the writing process, and that reason is publishing. Since some of students' writing time is spent on self-selected topics, you should decide how often they should publish. Some teachers say after the students have three pieces completed; others say five—you know your class and what is manageable. The students should decide for themselves which pieces they would like to publish. To explain the procedure, the teacher models this process.

Day One Publishing

The first day should be spent choosing, revising, and self-editing a piece of writing.

The teacher shows the class three pieces she has written and says, "Beginning today, when you have written three good pieces, you will decide which one you want to publish. First, you need to revise and self-edit the piece you have chosen. Next, find a peer editor to read and edit again with you. Then, sign up for a conference with me. Your finished pieces will be published in a book, so your classmates can also read your writing. Let's look at three pieces I have written."

The teacher reads and discusses the three pieces of writing:

The teacher puts "Lafe and the Cat Pool," "Collecting Poison Ivy," and "Merrill Kaye and the Wild Geese" on the overhead projector one at a time and reads them to the class. She says, "I want to publish something that everyone in the class would like to read. I like all of my stories and want to publish them all! Sometimes, this will happen to you. But, I have to make a choice. Which one is my best? Which one would more people like to read? I think I will publish the story about the time Alex collected poison ivy because we have all had experiences that did not turn out the way we thought they would."

The teacher returns to the chosen piece and revises and self-edits it:

"The first thing I want to do is revise and self-edit. I don't want to change much. Is their anything I want to change? Did I leave anything out? I think I will put a caret and insert where Alex went to art camp." The teacher makes a caret (∧) and adds **Tanglewood's** before **art camp**. The teacher then uses the Writer's Checklist to check her writing for items on the list. "I stretched out **mis-er-able** and circled it so that I will check the dictionary for the correct spelling of that word. You are old enough to use the dictionary to check the spelling of words you circled. On first draft, we don't worry about spelling words correctly if they are not displayed in the room. On final copy, every word must be spelled correctly!"

Day Two of Publishing

The second day, the teacher selects a student to peer edit her writing. The student comes to the overhead and reads the piece out loud. He asks the teacher any questions he has about the piece that are not answered in the writing. The peer editor wants to know if Alex went to art camp alone or with a friend. The teacher tells the class that Alex went to art camp with his good friend Chris. The student adds that sentence to the story with a different colored pen. The peer editor also finds another word that was misspelled (and missed on purpose) and corrects it. He thinks an exclamation mark might be more appropriate after the last sentence, and the teacher agrees with him, so he changes that, too.

Day Three of Publishing

Rewriting the story in final form. The teacher decides how to break her story into pages. In this lesson, the teacher has a premade book with 10 pages in it or she could decide that 10 pages would be an appropriate number of pages for this book. The teacher tells the class that one page is the title page, and the final page is for "About the Author," so she has to divide this story to fit on the remaining eight pages. She thinks about the length of the story and the illustrations she wants. The teacher puts page one at the beginning, page two where she thinks the next page should begin, and continues like this until she has it divided. The number of sentences on each page is not the same; she has Alex and Chris going to art camp on page one, the teacher giving the assignment on page two, Alex collecting leaves on page three, Merrill Kaye helping him on page four, picking poison ivy on page five, his sister and Dad helping press the leaves on page six, them covered with poison ivy and scratching on page seven, and the ending of the story on page eight. She then writes the sentences she has chosen for each page on the corresponding pages in her best handwriting. She can also type them on the computer. (If this is what your students are expected to do, you should model the process on the computer—especially if you can hook up the computer to a TV screen. When students have written long stories or chapter books this may take several days.)

Day Four of Publishing

The teacher wants to illustrate her book. This is a good day to read a picture book during the teacher read-aloud. She talks about how the illustrations in a book help the reader visualize the story or information. She then illustrates each of the eight pages. This may take the students more than one day. Usually there is more writing than drawing in the books made by students in the upper grades. The pictures make the books more interesting and give some students a chance to share their artistic talents, as well as their writing skills.

Day Five of Publishing

The teacher models how to write a page about the author (herself). "About the Author" is written about the teacher by the teacher, since she is the author of this book. "About the Author" is a mini-autobiography. She tells the class they can write anything about themselves that they think others would want to know. Do they play sports? Take dance lessons? Art lessons? This is what she writes:

> Mrs. Arens teaches fifth grade. She lives outside of Montgomery City with her husband, Jeff, and three children. When she is not teaching she likes to travel and give parties. Mrs. Arens also likes to write books. She has published two books for teachers and has written many books in school.

A simple cover is then made, and the book is put together and read one last time to the class (time permitting!).

Writing Mini-Lesson Focus: Grammar—Adjectives and Descriptive Words (Craft/Conventions)

Adjectives are parts of speech that describe things. Writers often "paint a picture" with descriptive words. When students use descriptive words to express their ideas or describe something, the writing is more interesting and will have much more impact on the reader. Key words describe how the subject looks, feels, smells, sounds, and so on. Similes and metaphors are often used in this type of writing. Mini-lessons on adjectives and descriptive words can often help students learn how to show, not tell, in their writing.

The teacher says:

"We have been reading stories and listening for descriptions. I thought it would be fun to use some adjectives and sensory words today and write a description. First, let's brainstorm some sensory words to describe our school cafeteria. Can you tell me some words to put under the headings: look, feel, smell, hear, and taste?"

The teacher and the class fill in this word chart:

look	feel	smell	hear	taste
big	hot	pleasant	noisy	hot
crowded	hard	spicy	chattering	crisp
messy	soft	sweet	muffled	mushy
bright	cold	pungent	quiet	creamy

Then, they write a paragraph or two together using these words to describe their school cafeteria.

Lunch in the School Cafeteria

Each day at school, I go to the cafeteria to eat lunch. As I enter the big, crowded, noisy, lunchroom, I see many people I know and like. The principal is standing there like a traffic cop, directing the students in and out. I walk down one side trying not to bump into any of the chattering students. When I hear the whistle blow, I know that is the signal for the red light to go on and the students to be quiet. From the kitchen, I hear the muffled sounds of the workers preparing the food.

As I look in that direction, I see the grilled cheese sandwiches, green beans, and salad waiting to be put on my plate. As I walk to my seat at the long table our class occupies, I sit next to a friend. I start with the crisp, green and red salad. Next, I eat my mushy, green beans. I save my favorite, the grilled cheese sandwich, for last. The cheese is still hot and creamy as I take my first bite. For dessert, I have chosen ice cream. It is still as cold as ice as I begin to eat it.

The teacher talks about the adjectives and the similes ("like a traffic cop," "cold as ice"). She encourages students to use adjectives and similes in their writing to "paint a better picture" when they are writing.

Other Ideas for Adjectives and Descriptive Words

Doing a Find and Replace Lesson with Boring Adjectives

Find (or create) a piece of writing with boring adjectives. Have students read the piece and identify the adjectives. Change some of the adjectives to make them more descriptive. Read the revised piece to the class.

Using Adjectives to Describe—Social Studies

Select a person (Benjamin Franklin), place (Alaska), time ("Gold Rush"), or thing (steam engine) you are studying in social studies. Model for the class how to write a description about that person, place, time, or thing. With word choices, it helps some students to draw or visualize before writing. Remind them to choose good adjectives to describe the person, place, time, or thing.

Using Adjectives to Describe—Science

During a unit on animals, insects, or plants have the students use adjectives and describe what an animal (insect, plant, etc.) looks like and also where it lives.

Using Adjectives to Describe—Art

Choose a piece of art (don't show the class) and write a description of the art—picture, pottery, sculpture, or jewelry. Have the students draw pictures from your description, then show the piece to them. How well did you describe it?

Describing People or Book Characters

Have the students write descriptions using adjectives to describe people they know or book characters they have read about (Harry Potter, Maniac Magee, Ramona Quimby, etc.). Then, partner the students with classmates and let them draw each other's descriptions.

Describing Places or Settings

Have the students use adjectives to write descriptions of some places they have been or special places like a lake or the beach. Then, partner each student with a classmate and let the students draw each other's descriptions.

Proofreading for Clutter: Too Many Adjectives

Find (or create) a piece of writing with too many adjectives. Have students read the piece and identify all of the adjectives. Decide which adjectives you do not need and change some of the adjectives to make them more descriptive. Sometimes less is better.

Giving Concrete Examples

Sometimes an example helps the readers more than the adjectives. Give students some concrete examples.

He was a hard worker, often working after quitting time if a job was not completed.

Using Similes

A simile draws a comparison between two dissimilar objects and uses like or as. Sometimes using a simile will help with the description. When you write for your students today, use one or two similes.

Amy wore a dress that was as dark as night. She could hardly be seen walking down the aisle, and she slipped into her seat as quiet as a mouse.

Mini-Lesson Focus: Grammar—Using Strong Verbs (Craft/Conventions)

Teachers often tell students to make their writing more descriptive by adding adjectives. Actually, a more effective way to make writing better is to look closely at verbs. Strong verbs are decidedly better for making pictures in your mind. A wonderful mini-lesson on using strong verbs is in *Craft Lessons* by Ralph Fletcher and JoAnn Portalupi (Heinemann, 1998) using Julius Lester's book *John Henry* (Penguin, 1999). It is a fine example of wonderful verbs. Use the term "mind pictures" or visualization—whatever is familiar to your students. Often, it is easier to "see" what is going on when avoiding passive verbs or even "-ing" verbs. One more resource with additional mini-lessons on verbs is *Lessons That Change Writers* by Nancie Atwell (Heinemann, 2002). The following mini-lesson takes on the task of strong verbs in an easy manner.

The teacher talks and writes:

"I have a sentence I want you to help me with."

> The dog went up the hill.

"I think the word **went** is very weak. In other words, my verb doesn't really help me 'see' this in my mind. Would you help me think of other words that would be better? What words could I use that would make this sentence stronger?"

The teacher works with his students to brainstorm a list of words to replace **went**. In many instances, this is not only a lesson on strong verbs; it will also introduce new vocabulary to some students. Some students would choose to say **went** because they don't know **trudged** or **scampered**. The teacher uses this time to talk about each of the choices and how the picture changes in his mind. Below are just some of the words students came up with during this lesson. (Allow your students to develop their own lists.)

went

trudged	frolicked	limped	lumbered	raced	ambled	sniffed
sneaked	rambled	dashed	loped	scooted	zoomed	slithered

The teacher talks:

"As you think about some of these new words, how does the picture in your mind change? I know when I say 'The dog scampered up the hill' I see a little dog in my mind—maybe a poodle or a yorkie. But when I think of **loped**, I see a lean, larger dog—maybe a lab or a doberman. The verbs you use make a big difference in your writing.

"Right now, I would like for you to copy our list into your writing handbooks. Write it just as I did. Put **went** at the top of the page and list all of these other choices. I want it to remind you of some of the possibilities.

"Then, write these two sentences."

> 1. Choose words carefully, especially verbs.
> 2. Make good mind pictures for my reader.

"Now, we are going to spend the next three minutes putting this into practice. I want each of you to return to your seat and choose one piece of writing from your folder. Read through the piece and find the verbs you've used. Are there any that you could change and make stronger? Try it on just a couple of sentences and see if you can tell a difference."

Other Ideas for Verbs and Word Choice

Using Words Other than Said

When students first begin writing dialogue, their writing takes a turn. Writing dialogue is not easy, and often a student's first attempts are not the best. The word "said" can occur so frequently that you will hear it in your sleep. Try a mini-lesson that echoes the lesson on verbs. Ask your class to make a list of words (other than said) that can be used in conversation. There are many, and your students will find more as they read each day. This is a great list to keep posted in the room, as well as in students' writing handbooks. A caution, however, is to not do away with the word "said" completely. In books, it is a commonly used word, and you don't want students working so hard at finding other words that they can't work on writing good dialogue. After you create the list with your students, ask them to look for more examples over the next couple of weeks.

Using Think-Alouds to Model Keeping the Verb Tense Consistent

By the time students are in the upper grades, they have learned much about the syntax of our language. Their knowledge is the result of natural acquisition—hearing and seeing good models of grammar and usage. For some students, correct grammar comes naturally. They may not be able to explain why certain words are considered correct, but they know which words to use. The correct word just sounds right because they have consistent modeling from parents, neighbors, and others around them. Other students have not had exposure to proper language usage, and they tend to write as they talk. This is fine for writing dialogue, but it is critical for you to model and expect correct usage to help students develop a sense of correct syntax.

Writing about the Past (Then)

Write a story about something that happened to you long ago and think aloud about keeping the verbs in the past tense.

> When I was eight I had (past tense) an orange, striped cat. We called (past tense) him Timmy. He looked (past tense) like a little tiger.

Writing about the Present (Now)

Write about something that is happening today and think aloud about keeping the verbs in the present tense.

> Today as we get ready (present tense) for our class performance we must remember (present tense) to speak (present tense) loudly enough for all to hear (present tense). We practice (present tense) so that . . . .

Making the Past into Present Tense

Write a story about an event in the past as if it were happening today (the first Thanksgiving, the Boston Tea Party, the sinking of the Titanic, etc.).

> The Titanic is (present tense) a beautiful ship. As I walk (present tense) from deck to deck, I admire (present tense) the ornate rooms and . . . .

(Be as forgiving as possible about the correct verb tense in writing in the elementary grades. The rules are complex and sophisticated, and there are so many irregularities. Criticism turns students off; modeling daily for students helps them acquire a sense of correctness through exposure to spoken and written language.)

Mini-Lesson Focus: Grammar—Nouns and Pronouns (Craft/Conventions)

A noun is the name of a person, place, or thing. A pronoun is used in the place of one or more nouns.

Students in the upper grades often know that a noun is the name of a person, place, or thing. They also know that, in school, they write about people, places, and things. Sometimes writers use pronouns instead of nouns. If you look at any sentence, the noun or pronoun is usually the subject of the sentence. Using the right noun or pronoun in a sentence can make it more understandable. During some mini-lessons, you need to focus on nouns and pronouns, just to make sure that students understand them and use them appropriately when writing.

The teachers says:

"Today, I am going to read you a page of the picture book, *The Velveteen Rabbit* by Margery Williams. (Western Publishing Company, 1990)." (A picture book has less text than a novel, therefore it is easier and more manageable during a mini-lesson.) "We will talk about and write the nouns and pronouns on each page. Notice that each sentence has a noun or pronoun as the subject of the sentence."

The teacher begins reading, stopping after each sentence, and asking the class for the noun or pronoun. The list looks like this when she finishes the first page:

The *Velveteen Rabbit*

Page 1		
	rabbit	he
	coat	he
	ears	his
	sateen	his
	stocking	he
	holly	his
	paws	him
	Boy	
	presents	
	Velveteen Rabbit	

The teacher discusses the nouns and pronouns found on this page:

"There are lots of nouns and pronouns. Most of the nouns are common nouns (rabbit, coat, ears, sateen, stocking, holly, paws, and presents), but there are some proper nouns (Velveteen Rabbit and Boy), too. Velveteen Rabbit and Boy are capitalized because they are used as the names of the rabbit and boy. Some of these pronouns are possessive pronouns, can you tell me which ones?" Together the teacher and the class find his, his, his, and him. They talk about how these possessive pronouns show that the coat, ears, and paws belong to the rabbit."

The teacher talks about the subject of each sentence:

The teacher and the class decide that the subject of the first sentence is rabbit. The pronoun he is the subject of the second and third sentences and takes the place of the word rabbit. The subject of the next sentence is Boy.

Add to the Writers Checklist

7. I have used appropriate nouns, pronouns, adjectives, and verbs.
8. I have used clear, precise, and underused words.

Other Ideas for Nouns and Pronouns

Using More Specific Nouns

See the lesson on powerful verbs (page 66). Write the same sentence about the dog, only choose one of the stronger verbs. (For example, write "The dog limped up the hill.")

Talk to your students about the picture this sentence creates for them. "Is it possible to change the picture again by making the noun more specific? How could I make **dog** more specific? I could write poodle, shepherd, or hound. I could even name a dog, such as Shiloh or Snoopy." Just as strong verbs make writing clearer to the reader, specific nouns can do the same thing. Remind the students that not every verb and noun needs changing. They should read each sentence and see if it would help the reader if the nouns were more specific.

Doing the Find-and-Replace Lesson with Boring Nouns

"I was looking through some of my writing yesterday, and I realized I used lots of boring nouns. I decided my writing would be much more lively if I replaced some of these boring nouns with more descriptive nouns. Let's read this piece I wrote about fishing, find the boring nouns, and replace them."

> When I was young, my dad always took me fishing at the lake. We would get up early and go out in the boat. Dad would put the bait on the hook, and I would throw out the line and wait for a bite. I liked to catch fish.

Try to use more specific or more descriptive nouns to replace lake ("What lake? Lake Norman"), boat ("What kind of boat? a motorboat"), bait ("What kind of bait? worms"), hook ("What kind of hook? fishhook"), and fish ("What kind of fish? rainbow trout").

Overusing Personal Pronouns

Because students often write many personal narratives, they fall into the habit of overusing personal pronouns, especially the pronoun I, in opening sentences. Unless you do a find-and-replace mini-lesson, the abuse will continue.

> I like to swim at the lake on hot days in the summer. I take my dog for a walk around the cove. I know he does not like to jump off the dock. I walk into the water to cool off. I know he will follow me in . . . .

(I like to swim at the lake on hot days in the summer. My dog and I walk around the cove. He does not like to jump off the dock. I walk into the water to cool off, and he follows me in . . . .)

The same is true for other personal pronouns.

> I went to Savannah with Michelle last weekend. She loves to travel. She was ready to go when I got to her apartment. She had called ahead for reservations at our favorite restaurant, Elizabeth's. She wanted to be sure she would not miss that treat. She had also checked the travel brochures and decided on a ghost tour after dinner.

(I went to Savannah with Michelle last weekend. Michelle loves to travel and was ready to go when I got to her apartment. Not wanting to miss out, she had called ahead . . . .)

Mini-Lesson Focus: Transitions in Writing (Craft)

Transitions increase the maturity level of writing. Students who just seem to "get" how to write will naturally include transitions. However, many writers leave them out completely, or worse, use only first, next, and last. There are many more options for transitions, and they occur in both narrative and expository writing.

The timing for when to introduce your students to transitions will depend on the types of mini-lessons your students need the most. It seems a logical topic to follow any work on paragraphing. If you use pieces of familiar literature to teach students about when to start a new paragraph, many of those examples will include transitions.

We are including a very large list of transitions. If that list is made available to students with no instruction, don't expect students to use the list. It will only be helpful and have meaning if they have been guided through finding some transitions and shown how using the transitions makes writing more effective.

The teacher says:

"Who knows what a transition is? Just now, when you came up here to join me for the mini-lesson our class made a transition. A transition is a way to move from one thing to another. So when we stop doing math and start writing, we transition from one to the other. For that transition, you put your math books away. You got out your writing handbooks and came to the carpet for the mini-lesson. Does that make sense?

"Well, today we are going to look at how writers make transitions in their writing. Sometimes it is necessary to move from one thing to another, and the author doesn't want that to sound choppy, so he might choose to use a transition. Transitions can be used to change the setting or the time or to compare.

"Let's look at a few of the books I've read to you as read-alouds. I want to show you some example transitions, and we'll work together to decide what kinds of transitions were used and why the authors might have used them."

At this point, the teacher makes overheads of a few pages from different books she has read. She finds the pages ahead of time and uses them only if transitions are obvious. For the first lesson, she points out the transitions and highlights or circles them to begin the discussion. (If your students have been told about transitions before, let them locate the transitions with you.)

Here are some examples of transitions:

Transitions

Time:	Early in the morning	As I
	While	On my way
	During	At 10:00
	Before	First
	Just as	Next
	When the teacher	At that moment
	Last	Finally
Result:	Hence	Therefore
	Consequently	As a result

Writing Mini-Lessons for Upper Grades: The Big-Blocks™ Approach

Compare:	Similarly	Yet
	Likewise	Still
	However	Nevertheless
	On the other hand	
Examples:	As an illustration	Specifically
	For example	For instance
Additional:	Moreover	Besides
	Furthermore	In the second place
	Also	Too
	Next	
Summary:	In conclusion	To conclude
	To sum up	In short
Emphasis:	Undoubtedly	Certainly
	In truth	Without fail
	Very likely	Obviously
	Assuredly	To be sure
	Perhaps	Naturally
	Yes	Surely
	Really	Without a doubt

Add to the Writer's Checklist

9. I have used appropriate transitions.

Other Ideas for Transitions

Having a Transition Scavenger Hunt

Once you've explained transitions and shown some examples, send your students on a Transition Scavenger Hunt while they are reading. By heightening their awareness of transitions, you will find students who are constantly pointing out the transitions in their own reading. Take advantage of this. Ask students to "collect" transitions as they read. They can be jotted on self-stick notes or on pieces of paper. During the next few days, allow time during the mini-lesson to add to the class list. Students can make copies of this list in their writing handbooks. It becomes a nice reference for transitions.

Mini-Lesson Focus: Modeling Revision Using a Think-Aloud (Craft)

Editing is proofreading for errors in capitalization, punctuation, spelling, grammar, and indenting. Editing requires knowledge of the rules of writing. Editing also requires students to scrutinize their work for application of the rules. While most editing is done after people write, they also frequently edit as they write.

Revision, on the other hand, deals with revisiting ideas and refers to the content and organization of the writing. Revision includes changing, deleting, adding, and reordering. As your students mature, they learn to reread and find appropriate places in their writing to revise. Since revision is an integral part of the writing process, teachers need to focus on revision during some mini-lessons. One of the best ways to work on revision is to write something with the class one day and then work on revising it the next day.

The teacher says:

"Yesterday, we wrote this summary of the book I just finished reading to you, *The Cricket in Times Square* by George Shelden (Dell Publishing Co., 1975). We wrote it quickly. Let's look at it and see if our summary needs revision."

> Chester, a cricket, travels from Connecticut to Times Square in New York City in a picnic basket. He lives at the Bellini's newsstand. He makes three friends: Mario, a mouse named Tucker, and Harry the Cat. They have many adventures and a few narrow escapes. Together they bring success to the newsstand.

"Let's look at the first sentence. I think it tells who the main character of this book is, Chester, and where he came from, Connecticut. The next sentence tells us where he lives in New York, but I think it would be clearer if we changed Times Square to the second sentence."

The teacher and the class read and discuss each sentence:

The teacher and the class decide to start the next sentence with Chester, not the pronoun he, and to explain in more detail who each of his friends are. They also want to tell where his adventures took place and write a better ending sentence.

This is their revised summary:

> Chester, a cricket, travels from Connecticut to New York City. He lives at the Bellini's newsstand in Times Square. Chester makes three friends: a little boy named Mario whose parents own the newsstand, a talking Broadway mouse named Tucker, and cat named Harry the Cat. They had many adventures in New York City. The story ends with the four saving the newsstand from bankruptcy.

Other Ideas for Modeling Revision Using a Think-Aloud

Revision by Changing Words

Sometimes, writers need to change words to make them more concrete and understandable.

"Do I need a different word for **said** or **nice**? Have we overused **I** or **he**?"

> Matthew said, "I see a big dog coming."
>
> "I thought you liked big dogs," his mother said.
>
> "I like big dogs if I know them. Once, a big dog came into our yard and tried to bite me!" he said.

These sentences might be better if they were revised by using a word other than **said** each time.

> Matthew yelled, "I see a big dog coming. "
>
> "I thought you liked big dogs," his mother said.
>
> "I like big dogs if I know them. Once, a big dog came into our yard and tried to bite me!" he responded.

Revision by Deleting Words

Sometimes, we need to delete a word because we have used it over and over again and it is not needed in some sentences.

> We decided to go to the musical on Saturday afternoon. When the day came, we went dressed in our best clothes and headed for the musical at the Stevens Center. The musical was <u>The Lion King</u>.

"In this paragraph, I have several words I can delete."

> We decided to go to the musical on Saturday afternoon. When the day came, we dressed in our best clothes and headed for the Stevens Center to see <u>The Lion King</u>.

Revision by Adding Words

Sometimes, writers want to add words (for example, the summary on the page 72) or sentences to explain more.

> I enjoyed the weekend at the farm.

After writing a sentence like this, students need to elaborate and tell why they enjoyed the weekend at the farm.

> I enjoyed my weekend at the farm. I had never milked a cow before. I like feeding the chickens, too. The best part was riding the horse in the back pasture. I got sore, but it was worth it.

Revision by Reordering Words

Sometimes, writers need to make sure that what happened first is written first, what happened next is written next, and what happened last is written at the end.

> We learned about North Carolina. First, we read about the coast. Next, we read about the piedmont. I liked learning about the Outer Banks.

"We need to reorder these sentences. The sentence about the Outer Banks should follow the sentence about the coast, then we can write about the piedmont."

Focused Writing: Writing to a Prompt (Craft—9 Mini-Lessons)

There are several reasons students need to learn how to write to prompts. Many state tests in the upper grades now include a writing portion or a performance event based on writing. While this writing may be more closely related to the genres you will study during your focused lessons, students may also be asked to respond in a constructed response or short-answer format.

Contrary to popular belief, the new state tests and other standardized assessments are not the only reasons to teach students to write to prompts. The most logical connection is in your content-area studies. It is only logical to ask your students constructed-response questions about their content-area topics. By asking students to respond to prompts, you encourage communication in the areas of science, social studies, and math.

Writing is thinking, and it is important for your students to sort out their thinking by responding to topics or prompts. It is also important, if you expect students to do this well, that you give them explicit instruction in methods for improving this type of writing.

Writing to a prompt or on an assigned topic is a task very different from the normal day in the Writing Block. Your students will be accustomed to writing for multiple days on their pieces, choosing their own topics, and often choosing their own genre. Therefore, it will be important for you to also provide opportunities for them to practice writing to prompts or assigned topics. The time you spend doing this during your Writing Block will provide practice in this genre.

Then, during content area time, you'll have more opportunities to ask students to think about what they have learned by writing responses to prompts or constructed-response items. Help students understand that there is a process that will benefit them. Model using the process and feeling comfortable with it.

Writing to a Prompt

Day 1: Generating a List of Suggestions for Writing to a Prompt

Day 2: Turning the Prompt Question into a Sentence

Day 3: How to Begin Writing to a Prompt

Day 4: Looking at Parts of the Prompt or Question

Day 5: Underlining Key Words in the Prompt

Day 6: Reading the Prompt to Determine Fiction or Nonfiction Response

Day 7: Self-Assessment

Day 8: Improving the Teacher's Response

Day 9: Scoring Your Answer

The following lessons are set up using the first day to determine a list of suggestions for making the process of writing to a prompt easier. The subsequent lessons are an extension or an opportunity to model how that suggestion works and improves student writing. If you decide to include additional or different suggestions for writing to a prompt, use your subsequent lessons to explain each suggestion.

It is also important to note, that while you may take a week or more to provide this instruction, your students are not writing to a prompt every day during that time; they are continuing to write on self-selected topics. Instead, you would begin with this instruction, and after you've finished the lessons, you might have your students try their first prompt.

On days students write to a prompt, your Writing Block looks different. It will be necessary to explain to your students that there will be no conferencing that day, as each person needs to be writing to the prompt and using a specified amount of time. However, in the week following the prompt writing, you might like to spend time visiting with each student and conferencing about her response to the prompt and how to improve her writing next time she is given a prompt.

Mini-Lesson Focus: Generating a List of Suggestions for Writing to a Prompt

Day 1

There are certain "rules" for writing to a prompt that improve the quality of the answer. While individual state tests may require specific instruction, in general, there are suggestions from which all students can benefit. Use this first lesson to initiate a list of suggestions or rules. Be sure to include any suggestions you need to use for your own state or standardized tests. If it will be the first source of instruction on writing to a prompt, you may need to tell the students the ideas to go on the list. If your students have been exposed to the idea of writing to a prompt, use them to brainstorm and generate the list with you.

The teacher says:

"So far this year, we have spent time thinking of things we want to write about, then you began your pieces and continued working on those pieces until you felt they were finished. Today, we are going to talk about a different way of writing. There will be times when I will give you a topic or a prompt to write about. You will be given a certain amount of time, and during that time you will write to the prompt or about the topic.

"You've already had a little bit of practice with this in social studies (science). Sometimes, I ask you to write a short answer or response to a question dealing with our unit of study. What you learn over the next few days will even help you do a better job of that.

"Today, I want to make a list of suggestions or rules that will remind you what will make the best response. Then, during the next few days, we'll take the time to explore and demonstrate each of the rules."

Rules for Writing to a Prompt

1. Turn the question into the first part of your answer.

2. Don't begin your answer with conjunctions (so, because, etc.).

3. Write complete sentences.

4. If the question or prompt has two parts, spend more time answering the second part of the question.

5. Use interesting or specific words.

6. Underline key words in the prompt.

7. Read the prompt to determine if your answer will be fiction or nonfiction.

(These are rules that will help any prompt writing. As you make the list, talk briefly about each item. Again, explain how this will help with things they write in social studies and science, as well as prepare them for writing on certain topics.)

Mini-Lesson Focus: Turning the Prompt Question into a Sentence

Day 2

One of the most basic concepts to use when writing to a prompt is to take the question and turn it into a sentence. Not only will your students avoid writing incomplete sentences, it will also help them avoid beginning with unclear pronouns (for example: they, it, them, etc.). Model for students the process of turning the question into a sentence. Be honest; tell them that it probably will involve a little more writing, but it will clearly determine the subject of the response.

The teacher says:

"Today, we are going to look at some sample questions or prompts. If you remember the list we made yesterday, the first item says we should turn the question into a sentence. Let's look at some questions we might be asked to answer, and I would like for you to help me begin my answer by using or 'borrowing' words from the question."

Who were the first Americans to move west? What were some reasons for the movement?

> They were pioneers . . . .

> The first Americans to move west were . . . .

"You always have to assume that the person reading your answer knows nothing about the topic or the question. Try to write an answer that will tell the reader the information he needs to understand the topic."

(You might decide to model a good response and a poor response. For example, with the choices above, you could explain that by starting with **they**, the reader wouldn't know what you had been asked or why you might be talking about pioneers.)

If you were Columbus, and you were given permission and money to take one more voyage, where would you go, and what types of things would you take on the trip?

> I would go to Australia . . . .

> If I were Columbus, I would try to find the route to Australia . . .

"Again, I have to look at the prompt and decide which words to 'borrow' to help me begin my response. I think my second choice is better because on the first one, the reader wouldn't know we are talking about the time period of Columbus; the reader wouldn't know why I am thinking about taking a trip at all.

"Remember to look closely at the question or the prompt and decide which words you should 'borrow' to make your response better. As we look at the second example, do you think there will be other 'borrowed' words before I am finished with my response?"

(Both of these examples will be referred to throughout the mini-lessons on prompt writing. Again, you may choose to use these specific examples, or you may choose released items or items from your content areas to model the process.)

Mini-Lesson Focus: How to Begin Writing to a Prompt

Day 3

This lesson works well with the previous lesson on turning a question or prompt into a sentence. Again, we are focusing on how to begin the response. Many students want to begin with pronouns or conjunctions such as **because** or **so**. This often causes students to write incomplete sentences or lose a clear focus.

Work with your students to create a list of words that you will not allow them to use as the first word in their responses. Think carefully about all of the poor choices you have seen through the years. The list below includes our suggestions. Don't be afraid to add additional words you have seen as problems. It is fine to add them throughout the year, too.

The teacher says:

"Yesterday, we looked at how you can turn a question into the first part of the first sentence of your answer. Sometimes, we can even 'borrow' words from a prompt to begin our responses. When we do that, it helps us make sure that our responses are clear. If we are not going to 'borrow' words from the question or prompt, then we need to make sure we still tell a clear message.

"Today, I want to make a list, with your help, of words we should not use to begin our responses. You may have talked about this before. If so, you can help me make the list. We'll keep this list up and even add to it as the year goes on. We might think of things today and then think of other things later in the year.

"Let's work together to make our list."

Words We Will NOT Use to Start Our Answers

Pronouns:

They

It

You

Because

So

"Cause"

(As you make this list, it might also be helpful to give examples of why these words make for unclear answers, incomplete sentences, etc. You could go back to the questions asked on Day 2 and try responding with some of these words. Be sure to use obvious, poor responses.)

Mini-Lesson Focus: Looking at Parts of the Prompt or Question

Day 4

Multiple part questions or prompts are often used. If this is the case, a good rule of thumb is to spend more time on the second part of the question than the first. For example, if the word "why" is in the second part of the question, it requires explanation. Spend some time looking at sample prompts and questions. Use this lesson to discuss the necessity of writing to the second half of the question.

The teacher says:

"Let's take a minute to look back at one of the prompts I showed you the other day."

If you were Columbus, and you were given permission and money to take one more voyage, where would you go, and what types of things would you take on the trip?

"As you think about this prompt, how many parts are there to answer? Let's underline the first part ("where would you go") and then let's double underline the second part ("what types of things would you take on the trip"). Looking at these two parts, which part do you think will take you more time and space to answer? Why do you think it will take more time and space to answer the second part?"

Who were the first Americans to move west? What were some reasons for the movement?

"This example is a good one to remember. When you read a question or prompt with two parts, it is a good rule to spend more time answering the second part of the question. It often asks for an explanation or asks for support."

"Looking back at this example, you can see that the first part of the question could generally be answered in one sentence. However, it would take more time to answer the portion on reasons why. In fact, just noticing that the second part of the prompt asks for more than one reason helps me see that it will take more time to answer that portion."

(All prompts have to be read carefully, then answered. Read these prompts with your students and decide what you have to do to answer each prompt.)

Think of a time someone when helped you, or you helped someone; write about that time.

This prompt requires students to write personal narratives with a beginning (which responds to the prompt), middle, and end. They should tell what happened with details and elaborate as much as possible.

You see a clown at the circus, describe the clown and what he is doing.

This is a descriptive prompt. Students are asked to describe a clown and describe something the clown is doing.

It is a new year. Will it be a good one? Why or why not?

This is a persuasive prompt. The students are asked to decide if they will have a good year and then elaborate on the answer and tell why or why not.

Mini-Lesson Focus: Underlining Key Words in the Prompt

Day 5

Many times, a student needs to be reminded of the important question words or how to determine words in a prompt. A good test-taking skill is to know those key words and understand the task at hand. Again, look at sample prompts, even the same ones used in yesterday's lesson (page 79). Work with students to underline the words that make a difference. It might be helpful to create a class chart of words to be aware of. Again, if writing some rules in the handbooks, have students make a collection of these words.

The teacher says:

"Yesterday, we looked at prompts to decide if they had one or two parts. Some of the words used to separate the parts are words we need to pay attention to. Words used in the directions again or question words set the stage for how you are to respond. Once again, look at the prompt about Columbus."

If you were Columbus, and you were given permission and money to take one more voyage, where would you go, and what types of things would you take on the trip?

"There are certain words that will guide my response. The question words are always ones to pay attention to: **what**, **where**, **why**, **who**, **when**, and **how**. These words tell you what is expected to appear in the response. You may also come across words such as: **explain**, **provide support**, **compare**, **show**, **if**, **summarize**, **evaluate**, or **use**. How will these words influence your writing? Why would it matter if you didn't pay attention to these words?

If you were Columbus, and you were given permission and money to take one more voyage, <u>where</u> would you go, and <u>what</u> types of <u>things</u> would you take on the trip?

"I think someone might not pay attention to the phrase 'If you were Columbus . . . .' To me, that phrase really changes how you answer this question. For example, instead of answering the prompt, some-one might write about one of the real voyages Columbus went on. However, this question is asking the writer to think about where else Columbus might have gone. The writer is not Columbus but is being asked to act as if he were."

(Students could be shown some prompts with poor responses that lack answers that address the questions. Have them help you decide which parts of the questions were not addressed.)

Mini-Lesson Focus: Reading the Prompt to Determine Fiction or Nonfiction Response

Day 6

Sometimes, the most difficult part of writing to a prompt is deciding if the answer is to be made up or if it is to be based on the knowledge of the writer. Many state tests will try connecting the topic of the prompt to a reading segment done in another section of the test. The prompt may ask for a fictional piece of writing, but the topic will be similar to a section of text the students read on the same test. Because this is so confusing, it is important to teach students how to read a prompt and make decisions regarding where to gather the information.

The teacher says:

"Yesterday, we looked at words in the prompt that would tell you what type of evidence you would need from a prompt. The words require you to do specific things. Another way to look at a prompt is to make a decision on whether your answer will be fiction, nonfiction, or possibly even fiction based on information. You need to make decisions about the type of writing you are required to do."

If you were Columbus, and you were given permission and money to take one more voyage, <u>where</u> would you go, and <u>what</u> types of <u>things</u> would you take on the trip?

"For example, if we look at this same example again, what type of writing will this be? Again, there are a few key words that allow us to make a decision. Look at the beginning of the question: 'If you were Columbus . . . .' Are you Columbus? Were you ever Columbus? No, you weren't. So, are you expected to know this information or will you have to make it up?

"Now, do you think you would need to use any information you may have learned before to help you answer this question? You would have to know at least a few things about Columbus to know what kinds of supplies he would take and how he made decisions about where to travel, etc. So, the answer for this would be fiction based on information."

Who were the first Americans to travel west? What were some reasons for the movement?

"If we look back at this example of a constructed-response question, we can, again, look at what type of writing is expected. Both of these questions ask for factual responses. The writer is expected to know the information and report it back in a factual manner. It does not ask for creation on the part of the writer. For this answer, you would stick to the facts."

You have just read a newspaper article describing a heroic rescue. You also read an excerpt from The Secret of NIMH, *where Timmy becomes the hero. Describe your own hero. Use examples of heroic accomplishments. Tell why you think this person is a hero. If you don't have a hero, tell what you think makes a hero. Why do you think so?*

"Now, I think this prompt is a little trickier. The prompt refers to the passages you've been reading. Sometimes, this will confuse the writer into thinking information from the passages is to be included. Why do you think the passages were even mentioned? Really, they are helping you to make a connection to the idea of heroism and giving you some examples of heroes. However, you are being asked to give a description of your own personal hero. That doesn't have anything to do with the passages you've read. It is information from your mind.

"An option is also given. If you can't think of a personal hero, you have the option to write about what a hero is in general. Again, you could make a connection to the reading you've done on heroism, but you've been asked to share your own opinion. This prompt is confusing because it mentions the reading, but the reading really serves to help provide some background knowledge."

This mini-lesson might take place over two days if you feel the need to model with more types of prompts and questions. It should also be repeated from time to time throughout the year, as students forget. Use questions similar to your state assessment, released items (if your state provides questions that are no longer being used), questions similar to the types you'll be asking on the tests you will give in the content areas, etc.

Mini-Lesson Focus: Self-Assessment

Day 7

Before introducing the idea of a rubric or scoring guide, teach your students to self-assess against the prompt. For two lessons (Day 5 and Day 6), you've spent time looking at key words and talking about the importance of using those words to make good decisions. One area most students can improve is spending time rereading the prompt and the answers they have written. It is important to find those words that direct the response and check the response against the prompt. There are always students who forget a part that they intended to include. Teaching students to reread for specific details and information will improve their responses.

The teacher says:

"We've spent a lot of time learning how to prepare to write and even how to start a response. Eventually, you know you will have written your response, and it will be so important to go back and reread. As you reread, look carefully again, at the words you've underlined and the portion of the prompt that guided your decision about the type of prompt (fiction, nonfiction, etc.). Check your answer against those words. Can you find where you explained, or where you gave examples?

"Rereading will help you check for the parts you know you need to include, it will also help you find other errors. Again, make sure that you not only reread the answer, but also the prompt. This takes time, and you will be tempted not to take the time once you've finished writing.

"Tomorrow, we will read responses I have written to some of the prompts we have been working with. I will ask you all to help me decide if I have addressed the portions of the prompt and if I have written the type of response I should have."

Mini-Lesson Focus: Improving the Teacher's Response

Day 8

In preparation for today, you will need to write at least two responses for the children to help you assess. It is possible that this mini-lesson should also be spread out over two days. Write to as many types of prompts as you want your students to be familiar with. Purposely leave out pieces the prompts ask for. Try to do the things you've seen your students struggling with as they write responses in your content-area studies, on state assessments, etc.

The teacher says:

"Today, I have brought in some responses to the prompts we've been reading. I need you to help me reread and check for all of the parts of the prompt. Also, I need you to help me decide if I've even written the right type of response."

If you were Columbus, and you were given permission and money to take one more voyage, where would you go, and what types of things would you take on the trip?

I would go to Queen Isabella and ask for permission to sail once more. I would plan to sail west again, but head further north once I crossed the Ocean. All of my other trips let me travel west, but I really began to head more southwest. Maybe if I go northwest, I will find Japan and China.

I will need a large number of ships, maybe 40 or so. I've traveled many times now, and I think if I have more ships and more people, it will make the trip easier. This will be exciting, I can hardly wait to leave!

"Let's read through my response and decide if I've answered all of the parts of the prompt. I need your help deciding if this is a good answer. First, let's read the prompt one more time and underline those key words. Can you remember what we decided for the type of response for this prompt? Will it be fiction, nonfiction, or fiction based on information?"

The teacher takes the time to work through the process with her students. She notes, "Even though Queen Isabella is mentioned in the first sentence, the response would be better if I'd turned the question into part of my answer. I did tell where I would go but I only mentioned how many ships I would bring along. What about the supplies? The crew?" The teacher works with her students to improve the quality of the response.

Mini-Lesson Focus: Scoring Your Answer

Day 9

For today's lesson, it will be most effective if you use your own state-developed scoring guide (if your state has one). Many states have scoring guides used to score the performance event for, at least, the language arts or writing portion of the state test. If this is the case in your state, teach your students about the scoring guide and let them practice deciding how to improve on their scores. Obviously, this type of scoring guide can only be used on the type of prompt that would require an in-depth response.

It would be a little different for a constructed-response type of question. You can develop a scoring guide or rubric based on the criteria you've established in these mini-lessons or even based on criteria you want to see in your students' responses.

The teacher says:

"In North Carolina, writing prompts are scored on a four-point scale based totally on content. Four criteria determine the quality of the paper. They are: main idea, supporting details, organization, and coherence. A conventions score (+ or -) for sentence formation, word usage, and mechanics is given to each paper, also. Let's look at my answer and score it together."

> I would go to Queen Isabella and ask for permission to sail once more. I would plan to sail west again, but head further north once I crossed the Ocean. All of my other trips let me travel west, but I really began to head more southwest. Maybe if I go northwest, I will find Japan and China.
>
> I will need a large number of ships, maybe 40 or so. I've traveled many times now, and I think if I have more ships and more people, it will make the trip easier. This will be exciting. I can hardly wait to leave!

"To get a one, a student must answer the prompt and write the type of writing that is specified. I did this. To move up from from a one to two, a paper must have clear, concrete ideas. My paper does. However, my piece is missing the supporting details and coherence to move it to a three or four."

> I would go to Queen Isabella and ask for permission to sail once more. I would plan to sail west again, but head further north once I crossed the Ocean. All of my other trips let me travel west, but I really began to head more southwest. Maybe if I go northwest, I will find Japan and China.
>
> I will need a large number of ships, maybe 40 or so. I've traveled many times now, and I think if I have more ships and more people, it will make the trip easier. We will need supplies for the trip. I will bring food that will travel well, enough for the whole crew. I will hire men who have traveled before. They will be hard workers and brave.
>
> This will be an exciting voyage. I will plan my list of supplies and buy them. I will hire the men I need. I will decide who will do what jobs and when they can rest. I can hardly wait to leave!

"Now let's look at the response after we read and responded to what I had written. The details and elaboration added would bring this answer from a two to a three."

Focused Writing: Biographies

The following is a collection of 11 mini-lessons to use in teaching how to write a biography. It is only a guide. It is not the way to teach the genre, nor should it be assumed that instruction in only these 11 lessons will guarantee that your class is ready for writing biographies. However, it is a guideline for consideration when teaching this genre.

The mini-lessons are set up over a four-week period, though the period of student writing is really three weeks. This approach also assumes that the class will be working on this genre as a group, rather than one or two students writing biographies at a time of their choosing. Either way is appropriate. Take what you can from this collection and make it your own.

Biographies

Day 1: Characteristics of the Genre

Day 2: Choosing Important or Life-Changing Events

Day 3: Developing the Character

Day 4: Inferring Traits of Characters

Day 5: Determining Questions to Define Your Story

Day 6: Creating a Matrix

Day 7: Matrix Continued

Day 8: Writing a Strong Lead

Day 9: Organizing Your Writing

Day 10: Using the Matrix to Write

Day 11: Writing a List of Sources

A list of excellent resources biographies to read to your students is also included (page 88).

Preparing for the Focused-Writing Mini-Lessons: Biographies

In preparation for these focused-writing sessions, the teacher may spend as long as two weeks reading a number of examples of biographies to the students. The examples should include picture books, chapter books, encyclopedia accounts, etc. Before learning how to write the biography, students need many examples to connect with. A bibliography of biographies to choose from is on page 88.

It is necessary to read more picture-book biographies than chapter books. Picture books are more similar in length to the type of writing your students will do.

	Mini-Lesson	Students	Teacher
Week 1	Lessons 1-5	Continue writing on topics of choice from writing folders.	Use the mini-lessons to write a biography; use conferencing time to ensure that students have good subjects.
Week 2	Lessons 6-11	Begin biography.	Mini-lessons focus on the genre and any topics students still need assistance with; conference to assist in the necessary stages of writing.
Week 3	Teach mini-lessons on necessary topics.	Work on biography.	Mini-lessons focus on whatever topics are necessary to move students forward with their biographies.
Week 4	Teach short mini-lessons on necessary topics to allow more time for conferencing.	Biography due.	Conferences should be publishing conferences; you will want short mini-lessons to allow more time to confer.

If the biography assignment is tied to a curricular study (for example: famous Missourians or North Carolinians during fourth grade, famous Americans during fifth grade, etc.), students should be made aware of this. They will need to make decisions for who they will write about. During the first five mini-lessons, students take notes each day, decide who they will write about, and find at least one source on their subjects. However, during this time, students continue to write, starting new pieces or completing pieces from their writing folders.

You will be working with the class to write a biography as a model. Much of the writing may be done in advance or in front of the class. In preparation for writing, read more than one source on the same person as part of the read-alouds. Choose from outside the realm of the assignment. For example, if your students will be required to write biographies on famous people from your state, have the class example be someone who is famous for a different reason.

Upper-Grades Biography Suggestions

Abe Lincoln's Hat by Martha Brenner (Scholastic, 1994).

And Then What Happened, Paul Revere? by Jean Fritz (Putnam & Grosset Group, 1973).

Bloomers! by Rhoda Blumberg (Macmillan, 1993).

Bully for You, Teddy Roosevelt! by Jean Fritz (Putnam & Grosset Group, 1991).

Can't You Make Them Behave, King George? by Jean Fritz (Coward-McCann, 1976).

Duke Ellington: The Piano Prince and His Orchestra by Andrea Pinkney (Disney Press, 1998).

Freedom Train: The Story of Harriet Tubman by Dorothy Sterling (Scholastic, 1991).

Georgia O'Keeffe by Mike Venezia (Children's Press, 1993).

Harriet Tubman: The Road to Freedom by Rae Bains (Troll Communications, 1990).

I Have a Dream: The Story of Martin Luther King by Margaret Davidson (Scholastic, 1994).

Lou Gehrig: The Luckiest Man by David Adler (Harcourt Brace, 1997).

Maya Angelou: Journey of the Heart by Jayne Pettit (Puffin Books, 1996).

Meet Maya Angelou by V. Spain (Random House, 1994).

My Great Aunt Arizona by Gloria Houston (HarperCollins, 1992).

A Picture Book of Abraham Lincoln by David Adler (Holiday House, 1990).

A Picture Book of Benjamin Franklin by David Adler (Holiday House, 1990).

A Picture Book of Harriet Tubman by David Adler (Holiday House, 1992).

A Picture Book of Martin Luther King, Jr. by David Adler (Scholastic, 1989).

Snowshoe Thompson by Nancy Levinson (HarperCollins, 1992).

The Story of Harriet Tubman, Conductor of the Underground Railroad by Kate McMullan (Bantam Doubleday Dell, 1991).

Teammates by Peter Golenbock (Harcourt Brace, 1990).

What's the Big Idea, Ben Franklin? by Jean Fritz (Putnam & Grosset Group, 1976).

Wilma Unlimited: How Wilma Rudolph Became the World's Fastest Woman by Kathleen Krull (Harcourt Brace, 1996).

Mini-Lesson Focus: Characteristics of the Genre

Day 1

During this mini-lesson, the purpose is to generate a class list of the characteristics of the genre. Having read many examples of biographies already, ask students to think of the characteristics of each book. If you have specific criteria that you want to appear in the final versions, make sure those criteria surface, either through your suggestion or a student's. Below is a list (not all-inclusive) of characteristics of biographies.

The teacher says:

"We've spent the last couple of weeks reading many different biographies. It is an interesting genre. It is a type of nonfiction, but it is usually told through a story, or a narrative. We usually think of most nonfiction as being expository, or more like a textbook. As we begin to write our biographies and learn about biographies, keep in mind that while you will find factual information to include, you will write a story about the person's life.

"Let's spend some time today listing some of the characteristics or types of information that you remember most of the biographies contain."

Characteristics of Biographies

* Dates of birth and death
* Where person lived
* Important contributions
* Important/life-changing experiences
* Character traits
* Fictional conversations
* Facts
* Details of family: childhood and adult
* Education
* Theme: why the author wrote the story

If there is time, you might return to some of the stories read and discuss examples of these elements. Be sure to include elements from the texts that deal with the person you will write about as a class.

Looking Ahead

You need to have read multiple sources on one person to be able to use that person in the whole-class examples. It is easier to connect with the students if the class example is written about a person for whom they all have similar knowledge. Look through previously read sources and find examples of those elements you intend to use on Day 2.

Mini-Lesson Focus: Choosing Important or Life-Changing Events

Day 2

Remind students that important, life-changing events were included in the read-aloud examples of biographies. You could discuss why the authors might have chosen certain events and what questions the authors would have asked. How did the inclusion of important events make the reading more interesting? (Refer to the list created on Day 1 if this is helpful.)

The teacher says:

"Yesterday, one of the things you said you noticed in the biographies I've read to you is that the authors included important events from the people's lives, and sometimes these were even life-changing events. For example, why did the author of *Duke Ellington: The Piano Prince and His Orchestra* include information about Duke Ellington not liking to play the piano? What question might she have asked herself? Maybe, 'How did Duke Ellington begin playing the piano?'

"Or, why did the author of *Lou Gehrig, The Luckiest Man* tell readers that Lou's mother thought he was foolish for quitting college? Why did he want us to know that Lou's mother thought sports were a waste of time?

"You will have to think about the different things you learn about your person. Then, you will need to decide which events will make the most interesting story. Some resources will share lesser-known facts about your subject. You will need to decide what is the best information to use."

Looking Ahead

In preparation for Day 3, think of other texts (read-aloud books) that develop well-rounded characters. You will want examples to be from a shared knowledge (explain) of text. You want students to relate to developing the character's traits, not just the physical appearance.

Mini-Lesson Focus: Developing the Character

Day 3

This lesson is adapted from *Reading and Writing Literacy Genres* by Kathleen Buss and Lee Karnowski (International Reading Association, 2000).

The teacher creates a chart featuring two of the students' favorite biographies:

The chart cites specific examples from the biographies that helped develop full, well-rounded characters.

Biography	Duke Ellington	Wilma Unlimited
Actions	"Whenever a pretty-skinned beauty leaned on Duke's piano, he played his best music."	"Wilma practiced them constantly, even when it hurt."
Speech	"The music of my people"	
Appearance	"Fine as pie good looks and flashy threads"	"Wilma's graceful long legs" "She was always so small and sickly." "Wilma stood tall and still like a queen."
What Others Say	"Duke Ellington's real instrument wasn't his piano, it was his orchestra."	
Thoughts	Didn't want to take piano lessons, thought baseball was more fun	"Ever since the day she had walked down the aisle at church, Wilma had known the power of concentration."

Together, the teacher and the students write statements (or paragraphs) about the characters described in the chart. The teacher asks students for feedback on how these examples help them know the subjects better. The class also discusses how the characters' actions told them more about the subjects than simply their appearance.

Looking Ahead

You will need specific examples of books that lend themselves to drawing conclusions (inferring) about a character. It will be most helpful if some of the examples come from the texts you'll be using to write a class biography.

Mini-Lesson Focus: Inferring Traits of Characters

Day 4

Give students specific examples from texts you have read aloud and ask how they help develop those characters in their minds. Choose sentences or paragraphs that require the reader to draw conclusions or infer. The conclusions and inferences help the reader develop a better "mind picture" of the character.

The teacher says:

"I want to read a few sentences from several different books today. They are all familiar books to you, as you've heard me read each one. I've chosen a few sentences that the authors used to help us get better pictures of the people being discussed. Listen carefully, and tell me what you know about the character because of the words."

The teacher reads the examples, then leads a discussion about what students know about the characters from the examples:

From *Number the Stars* by Lois Lowry (Houghton Mifflin Co., 1989), page 93

> "She remembered Ellen in the school play, moving confidently across the stage, her gestures sure, her voice clear."

From *Wombat Divine* by Mem Fox (Harcourt Brace, 1995), page 6

> "Emu was bossing and fussing as usual. 'Now, let's get started,' she said."

From *A Picture Book of Martin Luther King, Jr.* by David Adler (Scholastic, 1989), page 9

> "Martin was a good student. He finished high school two years early and was just fifteen when he entered Morehouse College in Atlanta. At college, Martin decided to become a minister."

From *Tuck Everlasting* by Natalie Babbit (Farrar, Straus, & Giroux, 1975), page 32

> "Winnie herself was speechless. She clung to the saddle and gave herself up to the astonishing fact that, though her heart was pounding and her backbone felt like a pipe full of running cold water, her head was fiercely calm."

From *Wilma Unlimited* by Kathleen Krull (Harcourt Brace, 1996), page 13

> "One Sunday, on her way to church, Wilma felt especially good. She and her family had always found strength in their faith, and church was Wilma's favorite place in the world. Everyone she knew would be there—talking and laughing, praying and singing. It would be just the place to try the bravest thing she had ever done."

Mini-Lesson Focus: Determining Questions to Define Your Story

Day 5

Look through the list of characteristics developed on Day 1 (page 89). Create questions to be asked in order for students to find the necessary information on the chosen people. If particular questions are required, be sure to put an asterisk beside those questions and make them a part of the writing assignment.

The teacher says:

"The first part of writing a biography is to research the information you will use to create your story. Hopefully, you all know who you will be writing about, and each of you should have at least one resource chosen by now. After you've done some reading about your subject, you will need to select some questions to guide your research, which will, in turn, determine your storyline.

"There are a few questions I will ask everyone to answer, and then you will choose three (the number is your choice) additional questions to answer. Let's look at some possibilities."

Sample questions:

When was _____ born?

When did _____ die? How?

What are the important events and experiences?

Why should I include them?

Is there evidence about what others thought?

What contribution(s) did _____ make?

What actions would help develop a more rounded character?

Could I create conversations to help with the setting and time of this person's life?

Why did I choose this person; what do I want to come out of this writing? (theme)
(This item is very difficult to address with elementary students.)

"Think back to the list of criteria we developed on Day 1. What kinds of questions would you have to ask in order to fulfill the criteria? Many of those questions are already listed. Can you think of others that should be included?"

Looking Ahead

For Day 6 you will display a matrix to begin gathering information on the person for the class biography. Decide on your format and begin to find multiple sources that will answer your chosen questions.

Mini-Lesson Focus: Creating a Matrix

Day 6

Determine which questions will be required, then choose the additional questions for the subject of the model biography. Begin to construct a matrix and model for students how they will find information and how they will put the information on a matrix. Ask students for different resources that they might use to find answers to their questions.

Use a pocket chart or large piece of butcher paper to create the matrix. Gather the sources for finding answers to the questions. Begin to fill in the information. See page 154 for a reproducible matrix. Make copies to give to individual students or make into a transparency for the overhead.

The teacher says:

"Today, I want to show you a method for organizing the information you will collect on your subject. This chart is called a matrix, and I am going to ask each of you to write your information in this way. You can see the boxes are small; this will help you remember to take notes and not write in complete sentences.

"You will also see how a question is answered differently by different sources. I will begin to fill out my matrix with your help."

Questions / Resources	When was Martin Luther King, Jr. born?	When and how did he die?	What were his most important contributions?	Were there actions to help readers know him better?	What did others think about him?
Biography Adler, A Picture Book of Martin Luther King, Jr.	Atlanta, GA January 15, 1929	MLK was shot in April of 1968	lead peaceful protests, fought for equal rights		200,000 people went to Washington with him.
Encyclopedia					
Magazine(s) Weekly Reader	January, 1929	He was assassinated.		Nonviolent	
Internet					
Videos March on Washington		Standing on a balcony of a motel, he was shot.		voice made you want to listen	People went to Washington because they thought he was right.

After modeling the use of the matrix, the teacher encourages students to begin their own matrices. Just finding multiple resources and writing in the questions will take some time. This may be a day when her conferencing time is used to monitor how the matrices are being used. It will be important for students to begin the process and use the process correctly.

Looking Ahead

Begin to write the lead, or several leads, for the class example.

Writing Mini-Lessons for Upper Grades: The Big-Blocks™ Approach © Carson-Dellosa CD-2427

Mini-Lesson Focus: Matrix Continued

Day 7

Model for students how to think about questions, read the information, and copy small bits of information onto the matrix. Don't write the exact words from the texts. Write enough information to help you remember the facts. Be sure to include the sources of information in the appropriate column on the matrix.

The teacher says:

"Today, I want to continue with my matrix. I mentioned yesterday that the small spaces help me remember to take notes. Since I am getting my information from other written resources, I need to make sure that I use my own words and not someone else's. For example, the text says, 'Martin was a good student. He finished high school two years early and was just fifteen when he entered Morehouse College in Atlanta. At college, Martin decided to become a minister.'

"How could I take that information and use it to tell about Martin Luther King, Jr.'s actions? What if I write . . . ."

Martin found school easy and worked very hard. He was smart and knew what he wanted to do.

"I have to write small and be able to convey what I have figured out about my subject. Let me do a few more before you begin working on yours today."

The students continue working on their matrices, and the teacher falls back into her conferencing routine. At this stage in the process, the teacher uses her conferences to act as both a coach and a guide. She checks resources with students and watches them in the process of writing.

Looking Ahead

Have several different leads written for the class biography. Students will work with you to decide which one is the best.

Mini-Lesson Focus: Writing a Strong Lead

Day 8

There are many ways to lead a reader into a story. A few strategies can even be named: questions, amazing facts, outrageous statements, starting at the climax. It is important to present models of many types of effective leads for biographies.

In fact, for the examples in this lesson use several biographies with strong leads. To help students focus on this genre, use only biographies to model leads for this lesson. Here are some suggestions: *Wilma Unlimited* by Kathleen Krull (Harcourt Brace, 1996); *I Have a Dream: The Story of Martin Luther King* by Margaret Davidson (Scholastic, 1994); *Bully For You, Teddy Roosevelt!* by Jean Fritz (Putnam & Grosset Group, 1991); *Bloomers!* by Rhoda Blumberg (Macmillan, 1993).

The teacher says:

"Today, we want to talk about the leads you will write for your biographies. I am going to reread several of the examples we've read in class, only reading the leads. Listen for the different ways authors chose to begin their stories. We've talked about leads before. Everything you already know can be used to write a lead for this biography."

The teacher reads the examples, then tells the class:

"Now, I would like you to listen to a few leads I've written for my biography. I tried a few of the techniques I saw in the books we read today. What do you think? Is there a reason to use or not to use one of these leads?"

The teacher shares the leads she has written, then gets the class started on writing:

"Right now, I would like for everyone to try writing at least two, if not three, leads for your biographies. We'll be doing a focused share at the end of writing time today where I will ask you to share a couple of different leads for your biographies. Be ready to explain why you chose the techniques you did."

Looking Ahead

You will be modeling how to use the information from the matrix to develop the narrative/expository text of the biography. Write at least a portion of the text ahead of time to use as an example.

Mini-Lesson Focus: Organizing Your Writing

Day 9

Lead a discussion with the students about the different ways authors choose to organize their information. Is one way better than another? How will you decide how to organize your biography? Here are a few examples of how to organize a biography:

Time Line (good for a book like *Wilma Unlimited*)

Birth . . . Event . . . Event . . . Event . . . Event . . . .

Snapshots (good for a book like *Bloomers!* or *Abe Lincoln's Hat*)

Not as focused as a memoir, but really more about one aspect or theme in a person's life, rather than a whole life story.

Flashback

Story begins at the climax and moves backward to fill in the missing information.

There are other ways to organize the writing, as well. Each student needs to decide which format will tell his story the best.

The teachers says:

"As you look back at the leads you wrote yesterday, do any of you have a lead that would determine the order your story is told in? For example, one of the leads I tried begins with Martin Luther King, Jr. being shot. What does that do for my story?

"In the example from *Wilma Unlimited*, the story begins with Wilma's life and tells her story in chronological order. In fact, many of the biographies we read aloud did that.

"When you are the author, you get to choose how to organize your information. You may decide on a different technique. Today, you will spend some time brainstorming the organization you think you should use to tell your story. Be sure to see if your lead has already helped you make that decision."

Mini-Lesson Focus: Using the Matrix to Write

Day 10

Show students the portion of the biography you have already completed. Demonstrate how you took information from the matrix and turned it into narrative or expository text. You used your own words; the matrix allowed you to avoid using the words from the authors of the resources.

Have students help you decide what to write next. Spend a larger amount of time than normal on this lesson. The class-written biography needs to be nearly completed during this session.

If necessary, you will complete the writing and use it during the next couple of weeks to model certain aspects that you are looking for or problem areas that you are noticing, etc.

The teacher says:

"Many of you have filled out your matrix and are ready to begin writing. The matrix is filled with information that you will take and turn into a story. That is not as easy as it seems. Today, we are going to spend longer than normal on our mini-lesson, so that I can demonstrate for you how to take that information and decide what to write. I also want some chances to let you help me decide what to write. It is a complicated process, and you can get some good practice on our class subject before you move on to your personal subjects.

"When I look at my section of the matrix that answers the question: 'What did others think about him?,' I see many different responses. I need to think about how I could show my readers the impression that Martin Luther King, Jr. made on others. I look at the strong feelings people had for him and about him, and I try to put them into my own words."

What did others think about him?

* Two hundred thousand people went to Washington with him.
* People went to Washington because they thought MLK was right.

  Martin Luther King had a way of connecting to people. People who heard him speak and knew of his beliefs felt better about themselves after hearing him. Martin empowered others.

  To think two hundred thousand people joined him in Washington, D.C.; he must have been a very special man. Martin Luther King, Jr. worked hard to spread a message of peace and equality.

"I read through the notes I made, and then I tried to put my impression into my own words. I have read many sources on Martin Luther King, Jr., and I believe that they all tell me the things I have written. But, I wrote it my own way.

"As you write your papers, you need to remind yourselves what you've found in your research. Then, spend some time thinking about it. How can you tell the story in your own words, based on the facts you've found?"

"Now, if your matrix is complete and you are ready to begin, remember what we've worked on today."

Mini-Lesson Focus: Writing a List of Sources

Day 11

Gather all of the sources used to write the class biography. Talk about the importance of gathering resources and then relaying the information from those sources to the reader. For this project, students will not be expected to have a formal bibliography. Model for them how to choose three or four pieces of information that you want from each source. Show students where to find each required piece of information as you model the format you expect to be used for the resource lists.

The teacher says:

"Today, I want to show you how you need to cite the sources you've used. If somebody reads your biography and wants to know even more about the person, the sources would give them a good idea of where to look for more information. It is also a way for the reader to verify the information you've used. If you claim to have written anything based on factual information, you need to back up that information with sources.

"I am going to ask you to provide three pieces of information on each source you used. For books, I want the title, the author, and the copyright date. You can find the copyright date inside the front cover of the book with all of the other printing information. For magazines, you can provide the same information. Web sites need to be listed completely, and if the site gives an author or related source, include that information. If any of you have used other information sources, see me for how to include them on your source page."

Title	Author	Copyright Date
A Picture Book of Martin Luther King, Jr.	David Adler	1989

"This is the information from one of the books, or sources, we used to write our biography of Martin Luther King, Jr."

(As with all other lessons, this is an example. It will be your decision for how to use the sources cited and even what information to have the students include. This mini-lesson could be held off until right before the due date. It is a final step in the writing.)

Other Ideas for Writing Biographies

In Fourth Grade

Have your students write biographies of important people in your state's history.

In Fifth Grade

Have your students write biographies of American presidents (or Canadian prime ministers), pioneers, or inventors.

If you are studying Canada, then your students can write biographies of well-known Canadians.

If you are studying Mexico, then your students can write biographies of well-known Mexicans.

For Any Grade Level

Have students write biographies of favorite authors, poets, or scientists.

After your students write biographies, have them try autobiographies.

Mini-Lesson Focus: Writing as a Gift (Craft)

When we talk to teachers about teaching writing, we always emphasize the value inherent in writing. When a person—child or adult—takes the time to write, he is showing you who he is and telling you what is important. For those of you who are parents, think of the little scraps of paper you have saved that your children have written on. Writing is valuable. For that reason, your students may want to think about giving pieces of writing as gifts. In *Lessons That Change Writers* (2002), Nancie Atwell provides many student examples of poems written as Mother's Day presents and memoirs written for Christmas presents. Your students have the power to give some unforgettable gifts. Teach your students about the power and the value of writing in May—as they prepare for Mother's Day or Father's Day—or earlier in the year for a birthday or other holiday.

The teachers says:

"I brought some things to share with you today. These are pieces of writing that were given as gifts. Have you ever thought about that? I thought that since Mother's Day is coming up, you might want to give some thought to giving a gift of writing to your moms or your grandmothers this year.

"The pieces I brought in mean a lot to me. My favorite piece is one my daughter wrote for me at Christmas. She wrote it when she was in fifth grade, and she wrote about her Mimi—my mother. Mother died in July, 2000, and Merrill Kaye and I both miss her so much. This piece of writing is one of the best presents I've ever received.

"The other piece I brought in is a poem written by one of my mom's students. This student wrote a poem about my mother as her teacher. I really do love the poem. It says a lot about who my mom was as a teacher.

"I even brought in some cards that mean a lot to me. I have letters and cards from my husband that he has written to me. Sometimes the words we can put on paper are the words we would have trouble saying out loud.

"Let's spend some time today thinking about the types of writing you could use as gifts."

Writing as a Gift

- poem

- memoir

- biography of the life of the person you are writing to

- collection of anecdotes or memories

"This is a great list. You can do this for any gift, not just Mother's Day or Father's Day. Your parents would love a gift of your writing for their birthdays or Christmas. Remember, if you write a poem, it doesn't need to rhyme; it just needs to let your mom or dad know that you love them."

Mini-Lesson Focus: Punctuating Dialogue (Conventions)

Dialogue is a very difficult craft. There are so many things to consider. While you need to model and teach your students about dialogue, expect to teach them again and again. Most of your students will know about quotation marks. The emphasis of this lesson will be to look at all of the other punctuation used with quotation marks and where it belongs.

The teachers says:

"I've noticed that lots of you are beginning to have your characters talk to each other. These conversations, or dialogue, require lots of work. There are many things to know about the punctuation marks used to show that people are talking. We also have to work at making sure the dialogue sounds real. Today, we are going to focus on all the punctuation marks needed to show that a conversation is happening.

"I think one easy way to learn about the marks is to look at an example of dialogue in a book. I chose one section from the book I've been reading to you (choose an excerpt that includes a good chunk of dialogue representing different kinds of punctuation). I decided to put it on the overhead so we can all look at it together.

"I want us to highlight all of the punctuation we see that is associated with the conversation. Let's use blue for quotation marks, green for commas, pink for periods, and yellow for question marks. Help me make sure we don't miss anything."

The teacher works with his class to highlight or mark all of the punctuation. He is sure not to choose a section that is too large, and makes sure that his transparency can be seen by the students.

"Now that we've highlighted the punctuation, let's see if we can work together to make a list of why each mark is used."

Quotation marks: go at the beginning and end of what is said

Comma: goes inside the quotation marks before a dialogue tag

                   goes after a dialogue tag if the tag comes before the words being said

Question mark: goes inside the quotation marks if the speaker is asking a question, even if the dialogue tag comes after the quote

Period: goes inside the quotation marks if the quote is the end of the sentence

                   comes after the dialogue tag if the tag is the end of the sentence

"This list will help us as we write dialogue. We will spend the next several days learning about how to use the punctuation correctly. As you're reading today, if you come across some conversation, see if you notice the things from our list."

Adding to the Writer's Checklist

10. I have punctuated quotations correctly.

Other Ideas for Punctuating Dialogue

Reviewing the List

Review the list created on page 102. Remind students of the different places you found all of the different punctuation. Glance back over the highlighted text as you talk about it. Now, model writing a conversation or a section of dialogue for the students. Try to incorporate several types of dialogue tags, creating the need for periods, commas, and question marks.

"I am going to write about a conversation I had with my husband on the phone. It was dialogue between two people, and I want to show you how I use the things we learned about punctuating dialogue to write this conversation."

"Hello, Amanda?" asked Jeff.

"Yes, it's me," I said.

"Where are you?" he asked.

"I'm on my cell phone, heading home from the airport."

Jeff asked, "Are you coming into town any time today?"

"Around noon," I answered. "Why?"

"Well, I left that contract on the books behind the couch. I was reading it last night, and I put it down there. But, I need it today," he explained.

"So, do you want me to bring it to the office?" I asked.

"That would be great," Jeff said.

Revisiting and Reviewing Dialogue

Review the list of punctuation (page 102) and look over the sheet that you highlighted. Ask for any questions or comments the students might want to make about the punctuation used in dialogue. At this time, ask each student to take out a piece of paper.

"Think of a conversation you had with a friend today. Write three or four sentences from that conversation, including the appropriate punctuation. Think carefully; this is your chance to show me what you've learned the last couple of days."

Collect these writing samples to find out what instruction needs to be reviewed or continued. After they finish the writing samples, ask students to spend five minutes rereading pieces of writing in their writing folders that had dialogue in them. Have students change any punctuation they think needs changing.

Mini-Lesson Focus: Using Commas to Separate Words and Phrases in a Series (Conventions)

Commas are important. In oral language, speakers use pauses to help listeners understand what they are saying. In written language, commas do the same thing for the readers; they signal pauses. Students in the upper grades have learned that it is necessary to use commas when writing words or phrases in a series. They often need to be reminded of this in a mini-lesson.

The teacher says:

"You know that words in a series have commas between them. Many of you have heard this since you started reading and writing in first grade. If you were writing about going to the movies with your friends and listed those friends, you would put a comma between each of their names."

The teacher writes a sentence as an example:

I went to the movies with Pat, Jim, David, and Linda.

"If you ate dinner at your grandmother's house and you wrote about that meal, you would put commas between the names of the food she cooked for you."

The teacher writes a sentence as an example:

On Sundays, we always eat dinner at my grandmother's house. She always bakes a ham, and we have mashed potatoes, green beans, corn, homemade rolls, and chocolate pie for dessert.

"Sometimes the list is really a list of phrases. Commas divide the items on the list, so that we can read it easily."

The teacher writes a sentence as an example:

Suzanne packed her new swimsuit, a pair of red shorts, a sleeveless T-shirt, and a lightweight sweater in case it got cold at night.

"We have to remember that the same is true when we write in social studies, science, or health. If we are writing about the cities in our state, the crops grown here, or listing famous people, we will have to use commas to separate words or phrases on those lists."

In North Carolina, the biggest cities are Charlotte, Greensboro, Raleigh, and Winston-Salem.

In science, we have studied electricity, the water cycle, insects, plants, and the solar system.

In health, we learned that the five senses are touch, taste, sight, smell, and sound.

"When you write today, remember to use commas to separate words or phrases in a series."

Add to the Writer's Checklist

11. I have used commas to separate words and phrases in a series.

Other Ideas for Commas (Series, Appositives, Dates)

A comma is used for many other purposes. Some of these your students may know, and others may be new.

Depending on your class, these lessons may be combined or done separately. If you do each one separately, of course, you will write more. The uses of a comma that are new to upper-grades students need several lessons and follow-up lessons.

Placing a Comma between the Day of the Month and the Year

On November 23, 2002, we moved into our new home. We spent all . . . .

Placing a Comma between the Names of a City and a State

My favorite place to visit is Chicago, Illinois. The city has wonderful restaurants and shopping. My favorite place to eat is on Rush Street where . . . .

Placing a Comma after the Salutation in a Letter

Dear Karen,

What are you doing for the holidays? I was wondering if . . . .

Placing a Comma after the Closing of a Letter

Your teacher,

    Mrs. Hall

Placing a Comma before a Coordinating Conjunction (new in upper elementary)

Chris wanted to eat the whole pie, but he knew it would make him sick. So he sliced off a large piece and began to eat it. Chris loved key lime pie and . . . .

Placing a Comma to Signal the Subject of a Sentence (new in upper elementary)

Even though the day was hot, we all decided to play tennis. We were hoping that no one would be at the tennis courts, and we would not have . . . .

Placing a Comma when a Slight Interruption Offers Additional Information (new in upper elementary)

Mr. Weatherman, the principal, was waiting to greet us as we entered the school. He took us to the . . . .

Placing a Comma between Two Equal Adjectives that Modify a Noun (new in upper elementary)

The basketball player was a strong, healthy athlete.

Mini-Lesson Focus: Using Concrete Examples (Conventions)

When writing, it is often necessary to give concrete examples to clarify. You might write, "Michael Jordan was not always a great basketball player." You clarify that statement for the readers by giving an example. "It is well-known that he did not make his high school basketball team the first year he tried out." This concrete example gives the reader a mental picture of just what you mean by "not always a great player." If you model this for your students again and again, they will begin to use examples in their own writing.

The teacher says:

"Today, I will show you how you can make your writing even clearer if you use examples. I am going to write about my daughter's dog. He is an Australian Shepherd, and she named him Aussie. Aussie likes to dig holes. He digs holes all over her backyard. He has dug up her rose bushes and other small bushes. Now, she has to fence in all of her plants. He digs holes to stay cool in the summer. When I take care of him, I usually take him for a walk. I do not walk fast enough for him so he ends up pulling me along. When I give you an example, you can understand just how much Aussie digs and just how fast he likes to walk. When we write, the examples help our writing just as they help when I talk to you. Watch as I write about Aussie without the examples."

The teacher talks and writes:

Aussie is my daughter's dog. We call him the "digging-est" dog. He likes to dig holes in her backyard. When I take care of him, I take him for a walk. I never walk fast enough for Aussie.

Then, she tells and writes the story again using concrete examples:

Aussie is my daughter's dog. We call him the "digging-est" dog. He likes to dig holes in her backyard. Aussie has dug up her rose bushes and other small bushes. Now, she fences in her small plants. One day he dug a hole so deep that we thought he was digging his way to China!

When I watch him, I take him for a walk. I don't think I ever walk fast enough for Aussie. I hold on to the leash, and he pulls me down the sidewalk.

The teacher tells her students that the sentence "He likes to dig holes in her backyard" needed a concrete example so she wrote two:

Aussie has dug up her rose bushes and other small bushes. One day he dug a hole so deep that we thought he was digging his way to China!

The sentence, "I don't think I ever walk fast enough for Aussie" also needed a concrete example so she wrote:

I hold on to the leash, and he pulls me down the sidewalk.

(Remind your students that when they write they may need to give some concrete examples so the reader can form a better picture of just what you are writing about.)

Add to the Writer's Checklist

12. I have included concrete examples.

Other Ideas for Using Concrete Examples

Writing a Paragraph and Giving Concrete Examples for Some Statements

Blue whales are the largest animals in the world. They grow up to 100 feet long and weigh more than 240,000 pounds. They swim in . . . .

"What is the concrete example for the statement: 'Blue whales are the largest animals in the world?' That's right. 'They grow up to 100 feet long and weigh more than 240,000 pounds.'"

Reading a Book, Writing a Paragraph about the Author, and Giving Concrete Examples for Some Statements

E. B. White writes wonderful descriptions. His description of the barn in his book Charlotte's Web is one of the best I ever read.

"What is the concrete example for the statement: 'E. B. White writes wonderful descriptions?' Right. 'His description of the barn in his book *Charlotte's Web* is one of the best I ever read.'"

Writing about a Student and Giving Concrete Examples for Some Statements

Patricia is a wonderful writer. Her writing needs little or no revision and editing.

"What is the concrete example for the statement: 'Patricia is a wonderful writer?' Yes. 'Her writing needs little or no revision and editing.'"

Writing about a Friend and Giving Concrete Examples for Some Statements

James is kind to his mother. He calls her each day to see how she is. If she needs, anything he brings it to her right away.

"What is the concrete example for the statement: 'James is kind to his mother?' That's right. 'He calls her each day to see how she is. If she needs anything, he brings it to her right away.'"

Focused Writing: "How-To" Writing (Craft—9 Mini-Lessons)

Traditional instruction on "how-to" writing has resulted in a paragraph form, including many time transitions, such as: next, then, before, etc. This paragraph, or collection of paragraphs, is to direct the reader how to complete a task in a step-by-step fashion. Often, students leave steps out or lack the organization to complete a piece of writing in a step-by-step, sequential manner.

The following collection of mini-lessons approaches "how-to" writing from a different point of view. It is important for students to examine the types of "how-to" writing they read and use in real life. The very first mini-lesson is a time to expose children, or often, remind children how they are led through a step-by-step process. In most examples, there are diagrams, numbers, letters, arrows, and other features to assist the reader in the completion of the process.

Likewise, teachers need to encourage students to choose a format that will best assist the reader in completing the task. The final product will then look more like the many examples of "how-to" writing gathered in these lessons.

As with most genres, this writing requires a lot of thinking and planning to ensure the process is sequential and well explained. It is important for students to think thoroughly about the logical order and necessary steps to achieve the desired result. In addition, students will want to consider features to enhance the explanation (drawings, diagrams, numbers, etc.). During the first two mini-lessons, students are still working on choice writing during writing time. After lesson three, they will begin to try the same step you model in the mini-lesson.

In this genre, the teacher will, once again, be writing her own piece to model the process. However, the teacher will be encouraged to write the same "how-to" piece using at least two formats and trying different features. When piloting these lessons, it seemed more students were apt to write "how-to's" that looked very similar to the teachers'. Therefore, the mini-lessons encourage modeling the same topic multiple ways.

"How-To" Writing

Day 1:   Many Examples of Real "How-To" Writing

Day 2:   List of Common Characteristics

Day 3:   Choosing a Topic

Day 4:   Planning the Layout

Day 5:   Planning the Steps in the Process

Day 6:   Writing a Strong Lead

Day 7:   Writing in Front of Students

Day 8:   Same Topic, Different Format

Day 9:   Comparing to the Scoring Guide/Criteria List

Mini-Lesson Focus: Many Examples of Real "How-To" Writing

Day 1

Gather your own examples of "how-to" writing from your home or classroom, or use the examples like the ones described below. Make transparencies of the examples to share with the whole class. Show each transparency to students. Discuss the features of each example. Point out differences and similarities. This first exposure to real "how-to" writing is just that, an exposure. Be sure to use examples using multiple features for showing the process (for example, letters, numbers, transition words, diagrams, etc.).

(Included are examples of a recipe, driving directions, bunk bed assembly instructions, computer game instructions, and building block/log assembly instructions. Attempt to bring a variety of "how-to" writing in as examples. Feel free to add your own examples that students might relate to.)

The teacher says:

"Today, I want to show you some different examples of writing. This writing all has similar purposes, even though each piece uses a different method for giving the information."

The teacher shows the class his examples:

Recipe:
Lists materials/ingredients first. Words in bold face show next step is beginning.

Bunk bed assembly:
Uses illustrations of the assembly. Uses numbers to guide the order of assembly. Uses illustrations to show pieces being used.

Computer game instructions:
Combines illustrations and text to work you through the start-up. Also uses headings to guide your reading.

Building block/log assembly instructions:
Uses pictures only for construction. Uses a guide on the front to show and label each piece and size.

Driving directions:
Gives step-by-step roads to take, distance and direction traveled on each road, as well as the visual aid of a map.

The teacher tells students the name of this genre of writing. She discusses the purpose of "how-to" writing—an end result/product. If the writing does not lead you to the desired outcome, the writing has had no benefit.

Looking Ahead

You will need these same examples tomorrow. Consider which text structures you want students to notice. Be prepared to discuss these with the class.

Mini-Lesson Focus: List of Common Characteristics

Day 2

On Day 1, the students looked at different types of "how-to" writing to find the different features of the genre. Continue the discussion to determine the appropriateness of the features for the specific type of task being performed. Students will need to choose their features based on the types of tasks they choose to perform and your requirements.

The teacher says:

"Let's look at these examples of writing again. Even though the writing all looks very different, there are some similarities. Can you help me make a list of the similar features?"

The teacher writes, listing the commonalties of the "how-to" writing examples from Day 1:

* Lists of materials

* Lists of tools, if necessary

* Diagrams or illustrations

* Pictures

* Used a logical sequence and a way to indicate that sequence (for example, boldfaced words, numbers, transition or time-order words, etc.)

"We want to remember these features and how they added to the writing. For example, in the recipe, I found it very helpful that the next steps were indicated by boldfaced words. It kept the recipe shorter; transition words weren't used. In a recipe, it isn't necessary to have a lot of extra words. Instead, it is helpful if the recipe is concise, or short.

"However, in the directions for installing/playing the computer game, I would want a full description and diagrams.

"As you begin to think about the task or procedure you will write, consider which features would be most helpful."

(If you are planning to use a rubric/scoring guide or checklist to guide your students, this is an appropriate time to share the rubric with them. Refer to it as you are writing your own "how-to". This will allow students to know the features required of them and the features that are optional.)

Looking Ahead

Be prepared to share a list of activities in which you are an expert. Have a real list you can explore with your students. Be sure to include things you could write a "how-to" piece to explain and things you could not.

Mini-Lesson Focus: Choosing a Topic

Day 3

Make a list of things you do very well. These would be your areas of expertise. As the list is created, give reasons how and why you know you do these things well. Explain that you really can't be an expert on something you've never done. As students are asked to write "how-to's," they might choose tasks they haven't really done, but that they know follow logical, sequential time lines. For example, students might write about how to make chocolate chip cookies because it uses a recipe, even though they may not have ever made the cookies themselves.

Once the list is completed, begin to look for ideas you could easily convey in a step-by-step process. Talk about each item and whether it lends itself to a "how-to" piece.

The teacher says:

"Today, I want to begin thinking about an idea for my "how-to" writing. I will have to choose something I have done and something I think I do pretty well. I might even consider myself an expert. If I am an expert, I won't have trouble explaining the process to someone else."

> Things I Think that I Am an Expert On
>
> * being a mom
> * making carrot cake
> * singing
> * cleaning house
> * taking pictures
> * hosting a party
> * teaching
> * ironing

The teacher makes a list of her areas of expertise, talking through the list as she gets each idea (or bringing the list with her to share with students).

"I think I am a good mom—you say I am anyway—but I know I couldn't just make a list of things you do to be a good mom. I think maybe it is more complex or complicated than that!

"Now, I could make a list of the steps to making a carrot cake, I share that recipe with lots of people, and I have had several people tell me it is the best carrot cake they've ever had. So, I'll remember that one.

"Singing is another hard one. It isn't really something you can list out, so that won't work. But, I do think I could give a pretty good explanation of cleaning a house, even though would take a lot of steps. I could explain taking pictures, and it would be important to show some good examples and some bad examples of pictures. I have both good and bad, so I know I've become better at taking pictures.

"I love to entertain, and there are usually steps I go through to host a party. My husband and I love to have people visit our home, and we usually have people tell us that they had a nice time. So, I think that is something I can do. That would be fun to write about.

"I love to teach, too, but there is not a list of things to do to teach. It takes a lot of learning and thinking to be a good teacher, so I don't think that will work either.

"Ironing might work, too. I know I can iron because I watch the wrinkles come out. But, it would be a lot easier to show someone how rather than to explain how with pictures and words."

After thinking out loud, the teacher makes a decision. She chooses "hosting a party." Once again, she tells students why she has chosen this topic.

Looking Ahead
Be prepared to begin modeling the planning stages of your writing.

Mini-Lesson Focus: Planning the Layout

Day 4

Think aloud with your students about the steps to map out a plan for your text. Remember, you will actually write this paper in at least two, possibly three, ways. You want to begin to think out loud about how the layout will look on paper. In other words, decide where illustrations and diagrams might be included. Model this on plain white paper. If students plan or write rough drafts on notebook paper, they often leave out other features. They are accustomed to what text looks like and, if not asked to plan for the other features of "how-to" writing (illustrations, diagrams, etc.), those features will be eliminated.

The teacher says:

"I have decided to write about the steps I use to plan a party. I liked the way the instructions for the computer game used words, as well as illustrations and diagrams. I think I could use some diagrams or maybe even some real photographs to show certain steps. Today, I just want to think about the layout on paper. When I looked at some of the examples from the first lesson, I remember how they used the space and labels carefully. How can I do that, too?

"This is just an idea for how it might look on the page. I will use both illustrations and photographs to help my readers 'see' what I am talking about.

"I also think for this example, I will use headings. I like the way the headings worked in the computer game explanation, and I think it might work for this, too.

"Before I go any further, I think I need to begin to plan the steps I will include in the writing, and then I will know which features will work for each step."

Invitation list

Menu

How to plan a great party

Looking Ahead

Begin planning the steps that will need to be included in your piece of writing. You will need to share with students the process you used for organizing.

Mini-Lesson Focus: Planning the Steps in the Process

Day 5

For this mini-lesson, you will walk through the steps you use to do the task chosen. Think out loud about the importance of order, when it is important, and the necessity of including every single step. Decide whether the step itself is enough explanation or if it needs further information. Use the examples from the first lesson to show the differences.

The computer game directions have headings that name the steps. However, there is also additional text to explain each step. In contrast, the recipe states each step and moves on to the next; no further explanation is needed. Which kind of writing best suits the task you have chosen?

The teacher says:

"My task, planning a party, is a little more like the computer game directions. I think I am going to need to explain each step with more information. Some of the steps may be self-explanatory, but I know I will have to explain others. That is why I think headings will work for my piece. But today, my job is to decide what the steps in the process are.

"I know I always begin by choosing a date, at least three weeks away, and creating a guest list. Maybe I'll just write these steps on a list and then decide how to write details about each one."

Planning a Party

1. Choose a date (at least three weeks in advance).

2. Decide who to invite.

3. Select a menu.

4. Choose flowers or decorations.

I do items 2, 3, and 4 several days in advance.

5. Cook the food.

6. Clean the house.

7. Get myself ready.

8. Put out food and drinks.

9. Light candles.

10. Turn music on.

11. Welcome the guests!

Looking Ahead

Tomorrow, you will talk to students about appropriate leads for this piece of writing. Develop at least three that will work well for your topic.

Mini-Lesson Focus: Writing a Strong Lead

Day 6

Share the three leads that you wrote with the class. Talk about how you developed each lead. You might use an interesting fact, make a connection to why you and others might enjoy doing this task, or ask a question. After sharing your three examples, share examples you will not allow anyone to use:

"I am going to show you how to plan a party."

"I am going to tell you how to have a great party."

"Hi, my name is Mrs. Arens, and I'm going to tell you how to plan a party."

These leads are not acceptable because they do not accomplish the task of a good lead—to draw the reader in. No one will be starting a paper in this way.

The teacher says:

"I've written three leads to start my piece. I want to share those with you today and see what you think. I also want to share some leads with you that I won't let anyone use. Just like anything else we've written, it is really important to write an appropriate lead. "

Going to a good party is a lot of fun. Hosting a good party can be a lot of fun, too. However, it takes time and energy. I find that I always use the same process. I hope you will find this guide to planning a great party helpful.

Have you ever been to a great party and wondered how the host ever had time to think of all the details? Well, I would like to show you the steps I take to make sure my guests feel comfortable. Here is how you can learn to host a great party, too.

Having a great party is like writing a great paper—it takes a lot of planning. On the other hand, the planning can be a lot of fun. These are some suggestions for planning a great party so that you and your guests will be comfortable and can concentrate on enjoying yourselves.

"Which lead do you like best? Why are these better choices than the lead 'I am going to show you how to plan a party'?"

The teacher gives students the chance to practice their own leads with topics from the expert lists they created on Day 3. She incorporates time for each student to share his leads with a partner or two and encourages feedback.

Looking Ahead

For tomorrow's lesson, you will either begin the actual writing of your piece or bring what you have already written so far and add to it in front of the students. Either way is fine, as long as you write in front of them during the mini-lesson.

Mini-Lesson Focus: Writing in Front of Students

Day 7

Either using the planning you've done so far, or the piece you've written outside of class, show students how you go back to the steps you planned to decide what to write next. Talk and think aloud about all of the decisions you make on explanations, text structures, placement on the page, etc.

The teacher says:

"I began writing my piece yesterday while you were working on leads. I want to show you what I have so far, and I'll add to it, today. I have found it very helpful to have my list of steps and my planning sheet with me to refer to.

"You all helped me choose a lead yesterday, and I knew the first couple of steps. I also had my diagrams of a guest list and a menu plan. I knew my first explanations had to include that information.

"Now, this is what I have so far, and I can see I won't be able to get my illustration of the menu on this page as I had planned. I had too much to explain in the process. Now, I'm ready to explain the next step. I want you to watch how I use all of my planning to help."

The teacher refers to the planning she has done and continues to write in front of the students on her chosen topic. (Don't spend too much time as it takes away from students' writing time.)

How to Plan a Great Party

Having a great party is like writing a great paper—it takes lots of planning. The planning can be a lot of fun. These are some suggestions for planning a great party so that you and your guests will be comfortable and can concentrate on enjoying yourselves.

The first few steps need to be taken care of well in advance, at least three weeks prior to the event. The other steps happen a few days before, and finally, there are preparations the day of the party.

Setting the Date

The first step is choosing a date that seems to be open for you, the host, and for many of the people you plan to invite. The date should be at least three weeks away in order to have time to mail the invitations, give the guests the chance to respond, and make plans.

When deciding who to invite, you must consider how many people you want to entertain. A good rule to remember is that 50 - 75% of the guest list will be able to attend. Don't invite more than you can handle, spacewise or foodwise.

It is a good idea to look through the guest list and make sure that there are groups of people or couples who you know are good friends. They will all be friends and acquaintances of yours, but being the host, you will not be able to visit with them the whole time.

Make sure that you have addresses or phone numbers of the people on your list, depending on whether you will mail the invitations or phone the guests.

Looking Ahead

Be prepared to show your students another format using the same topic tomorrow. See page 116 for an example.

Mini-Lesson Focus: Same Topic, Different Format

Day 8

This mini-lesson focuses on the same topic as Day 7 written in a different format. It is designed to look much like the recipe described on page 109. Have students compare today's writing with the other format. Ask them questions like, "Which is more suitable for the topic? Why do you think so? Is today's example explicit enough? Does the format depend on your experience level?"

Use this mini-lesson to show students that the same topic can be covered in many ways. Encourage them to decide which formats will be most user-friendly for their chosen topics.

The teacher says:

"I have written my process for planning a party again, but this time I've done it in a very different manner. I tried to use a similar layout and format to the recipe we looked at. One of the things I thought about is: if I used this as my format, it would need to be for someone who already knows about hosting a party, but wants just a few new ideas."

How to Host a Great Party

Materials:
Guest list
Menu
Invitations and addresses, or phone numbers
Groceries
A clean house

Write a list of the people you want to invite, at least three weeks ahead of time. Mail invitations or call each person on the list. Decide what food and drinks you will be serving. Go to the grocery store and get the ingredients about two days ahead of the party. Make any food that can be made ahead of time. Prepare the other foods on the day of the party. Clean your house. Get yourself ready. Put out the food and any decorations or flowers. Light candles and turn on music. Prepare to greet your guests.

Looking Ahead

For Day 9, you will be reviewing a completed "how-to" that you have written. Make sure you have a complete piece to check the steps.

Mini-Lesson Focus: Comparing to the Scoring Guide/Criteria List

Day 9

Start the mini-lesson by reading through your paper. As you read through, think aloud about how the examples, the steps, and the explanations you used would help someone actually complete this task. If you have forgotten steps, model how you would add them or discuss with the class whether you think it is necessary to include this information.

If you want to add one more dimension to the writing, have each student determine if he should include a level. In other words, would the "how-to" piece be for a beginner or is it written for someone who has had some experience with the task.

If you have developed a scoring guide, model checking your paper against the scoring guide. Or, at least compare it to a list of criteria you have developed for requirements.

The teacher says:

"Now that I have my finished my writing, I need to go back to the scoring guide (or checklist) that lists the criteria I need. I would like you to help me decide what needs work and what seems to be okay."

The teacher works through the process with the students watching. (It might be helpful, if you are using a rubric, to intentionally write a paper that would score lower in an area or two. That would allow you to model the process of deciding how to improve in those areas. This may be a longer lesson, or you might want to go more than one day.)

Focused Writing: Informational Text (Craft—8 Mini-Lessons)

The Writing Block exists for several purposes in a classroom. As emergent readers develop, many will learn to read by writing. Teachers teach young children to use writing as a way of telling something. As students get older and their reading abilities increase, teachers also want them to see writing as a method for sharing and thinking about what they know.

The infamous report has been a school genre for many years. Nancie Atwell (*Lessons That Change Writers*, 2002) encourages teachers to move away from the genres that exist only in schools between the hours of 8:00 A.M. and 3:00 P.M. A report is not something found in libraries, at least not the type of report teachers assign to students.

Perhaps another problem with the report is that students are told to do research and are given no instruction. How will students learn to do research in this way? Another factor to consider is the age appropriateness of research. Researching is a complicated process: deciding what information to gather, gathering the information, then turning the information into your own words. Therefore, young students will need to experience research in a guided assignment before being asked to carry out the task independently.

There has been a recent push in elementary classrooms to share and encourage more reading of nonfiction texts. What kinds of books do you think of when you think of nonfiction? Do those texts look anything like the reports your students have written? Most often, you see the regurgitated report that sounds similar to the classroom encyclopedia or the text found on your students' favorite Web sites.

In many of the other focused genres, it is necessary to read many examples prior to the instruction for writing. For writing informational text, the task is twofold. Not only do the students need a large repertoire of informational/nonfiction text to fall back on, they will also need a large amount of knowledge on the topics they choose to research.

The process of researching is much easier when the researcher has a body of knowledge to work with. It is very difficult to do the research at the same time the writer learns about the topic for the first time. Without knowing about the given topic, it is hard to know what questions to ask and what information to share.

During the mini-lessons in this focused genre, you will be modeling how to write a piece of informational text. Therefore, it will be helpful to choose a topic to model that your students have already been studying and that you have been reading additional information about.

Consider the simple process of using a KWL chart. If a topic of study begins with filling out the KWL, the items in the "Know" column will often include misinformation. As the teacher, you are assuming that any knowledge students have on the topic is current and correct. Then, you immediately move on to the "Want to know" column. Students' questions for this column seem to be surface-level at best, and many of them don't know what to ask.

However, if you begin a unit of study by reading aloud some basic background information to students about the topic, their knowledge for the "Know" column has already begun developing. Furthermore, the basic learning often stimulates students to want to know more. The "Want to know" column is filled with more questions, and most of them will be answerable.

This same theory applies to teaching students how to do research. If students are choosing topics at the same time the writing begins, don't be surprised if no reading occurs; often students are only skimming for information. They will gather the information in bits and pieces. Transferring these bits and pieces into expository text is very difficult.

Many of your students will have written nonfiction pieces prior to this instruction in research. If you have not seen these pieces in your classroom, ask teachers of the primary grades to share with you. The pieces of nonfiction written by emergent and early writers come from knowledge—not from research. Students who know a lot about snakes write about snakes. Many classrooms will house a car-mechanic expert or a motorcycle-racing expert. These students don't need to do research because they already know so much.

When these experts begin to write, the process is not difficult because they are writing about things they know. Consequently, your students will be more successful with informational writing if they first become experts through reading.

Consider doing the first two mini-lessons a full two or three weeks prior to the rest of the lessons. Encourage students to choose topics of interest related to a content area of study and find multiple resources on those topics. In fact, it would be okay if you finish, or nearly finish, the content study before the writing begins. This will ensure a basic level of knowledge for all students and give them a chance to choose their pieces of content. Allow (and require) students to read the texts before developing questions or taking notes on the material.

	Mini-Lesson	Students	Teacher
Weeks 1 and 2 (possibly 3)	Lessons 1-2	Choose topic and select resources to be read during Self-Selected Reading, subject-area time, and at home. Writer's Workshop continues.	Use mini-lessons to model choosing a topic and selecting materials; teach regular mini-lessons while students read and research their topics.
Week 3	Lessons 3-7	Work on the aspects modeled in the mini-lesson; taking notes will take longer than it takes to model.	Spend time conferencing with students while they are writing to help head off any major problems.
Week 4	Lesson 8	Work on research and writing; conference with the teacher.	After Day 8 on features, continue with short review mini-lessons to allow more time to conference.

Informational Text

Day 1: Choosing a Topic

Day 2: Selecting Materials

Day 3: How to Do Research

Day 4: Taking Notes

Day 5: Formatting the Text

Day 6: Organizing the Information

Day 7: Paragraphs

Day 8: Features of Nonfiction Text

This focused writing on informational text is a natural tie-in to the content areas. The general topic is coordinated with the area of study; however, students are allowed to specify within the topic for their own writing. For example, if you are doing a unit on space, the students might be asked to write about planets, or to choose other concepts from your unit.

Mini-Lesson Focus: Choosing a Topic

Day 1

It is crucial for students to choose well when they select their topics. If there is no interest, the student will not be motivated to read and then share what was discovered. For this reason, you still need to embed a bit of choice in the research. While you will generally determine the umbrella topic, the students should have choice within that unit of study.

If this is the first introduction to research, it might be a good idea to leave the topic very open-ended. In other words, don't feel compelled to tie this research into your content area. Teach the concept of research and writing expository text with a topic of student choice. Once they have had the experience and have a basic understanding of research, tie it into content studies.

The teacher says:

"We are going to be doing some research in a couple of weeks. After we do the research, we will write about what we learned. Who knows what it means to do research? (Expect at least a little bit of class discussion on this.) Right, it is a way of finding out more about a topic. The part we have to do before we write about what we learned is find some resources that will help us learn.

"Today, I want to talk to you about choosing your topics. I know that most of you have probably written on something you feel you're an expert on. (If you've already written a "how-to" piece, connect to that piece of writing.) When you have a lot of knowledge about something, you become an expert on that topic. I know all of you have some interests that you know more about than I do. We've talked all year about how it is always easier to write about things you know, than it is to write about something you are not sure of or something you are making up.

"As we prepare to do this research, I want you to become experts first. We won't even talk about the process of this type of writing for another two weeks or so. During the two weeks, you will choose your topics, find your resources, and commit yourselves to reading about your interests. During that time, your reading will build your expertise, and I think that will make the writing so much easier for you."

(The next part of your mini-lesson will be determined by the way you will use this research. If you plan to allow students to choose any topic, you need to talk about choosing an area of expertise and how to further the knowledge. If your research will tie in to a content area and a general topic, set the parameters for how students will select a topic within that area. The script that follows assumes the research will align with a content area study.)

"In science, we have been studying mammals. You all have a good understanding of the characteristics of mammals. When we begin our research writing, I am going to ask each of you to choose a mammal. So today, your job is to think about a mammal that you either know a lot about, and would like to know more about, or a mammal that you think is interesting and don't know much about. Whether you already know a lot about that mammal or not, you will be asked to choose multiple resources and read about that mammal.

"My job is to help you find multiple resources to read. Probably our biggest challenge is to find sources that you are able to read and find interesting or engaging. I am going to ask you to apply a focus to this topic. In other words, if I choose the elephant as my mammal, I will quickly find that there are two different types of elephant: African and Asian. To make my job as the researcher easier, I will decide right away which of those elephants I want to know more about. Elephants provide a limited choice—there are only two. Some of you may choose mammals that offer many more choices. Narrow your topic as soon as possible. It will help you read more efficiently and become an expert in a specific field.

"It is now time for you to do some thinking. Our writing time today will be spent making decisions. If it helps you to brainstorm possibilities on paper, feel free to do that. If you would rather do some quiet thinking, that is an option as well.

"I ask that you submit your topic to me in writing. I want to compile a list of topics to give to our librarian, and I want to be able to go to the public library and find more resources. I also want to check out any of my personal resources that I might be able to bring in for us to use.

"Use your time wisely today and bring your topic to me when you have it. I will try to find time to at least check in with each of you today, as I learn your interest. If you finish choosing your topic and have additional time, go back to the work you have in your writing folder."

(The language used in this mini-lesson is specific. Not only does it tell students to narrow their focus as soon as possible, it also tells you to use as many resources as possible. It will be critical to find low-level resources for your students who need them. Think of every possible place. If you want to include Internet resources, assist students in finding the Web sites and print the pages of information. The next two weeks should include time for reading because you want the text in the students' hands. Avoid the need to "go to the computer lab" instead of reading for information. Make it a goal to get resources into the students' hands by the end of the next day or two. Their interests will be highest at the time they select their topics.)

Mini-Lesson Focus: Selecting Materials

Day 2

If you choose to encourage students in choosing the materials they will use, use this mini-lesson to model how to make the decision. Build on the strategies you have shared with students for choosing books but with modifications. Some of the materials they choose may be rather difficult. However, think about all of the features of text they could learn from: headings, diagrams, maps, charts, labels, photographs, etc. Even if the running text is difficult, there could be other features the students could use to increase their knowledge.

The teacher says:

"Let's brainstorm or at least think about the different places we might look for information on your mammals. What are some places you might look? (Work with students to create a list and feel free to add to the list and comment on recommendations.) Think about the type of reading you have done when you learned facts or information.

Encyclopedia
"Okay, this is a good resource for information. I think you might find it is really hard to read, but it would be one place to find some facts."

Internet
"This is another good source, and I have a list of some Web sites that will give you good information on mammals. When you find the information you want, you will print that information and keep it with everything else you will be reading."

Books
"Great idea. Many of you will find whole books written on the mammals you chose. Another way to think about books is to think of the areas you would find the animals and look for books that might include some information on your topics. Going back to my idea of elephants, I want to research the African elephant, so I might look for a book on Africa or on African elephants. If you choose a mammal that is a pet, you might find more information about that animal in a book on pets. Does that make sense?"

Magazines
(If this doesn't come up, bring it up yourself.) "These are great resources. Think about some of the magazines we've read this year. *Students Discover, National Geographic World, Zoo Books* are all magazines that might give us information. There could be issues dealing with the topics you've chosen. I will help you look for issues if you are not sure."

(As you work through this list, you may have students mention reasonable resources that don't involve reading—videos, interviews, etc. Affirm the students in knowing these are valuable resources and resources you will eventually use. Today's task is to think of resources involving reading.)

"Let's head to the library (or wherever you will take them) and begin our search for materials. Keep in mind the different resources you've mentioned. The librarian and I will be there to help you in your search."

(Searching the library for materials is a tough task. Ask your librarian and any other staff that might be available for help. Students who are not having success finding the needed resources will quickly get off-task and make the library trip a management nightmare. Do as much as you can ahead of time to make the trip a "gold mine" of information.)

Mini-Lesson Focus: How to Do Research

Day 3

In this mini-lesson, you will teach students how to formulate questions. If you plan to require students to answer certain questions, you will need to present those questions at this time. For the sake of interest and motivation, you might choose a small number of required questions and allow for a couple of choices. Frequently remind students to think about what they know. Both important and interesting facts should be included.

The teacher says:

"You have been reading about your mammals for a couple of weeks now, and I hope you feel like you've learned a lot in that time. I know I've learned more about elephants in the reading I've done. Today, we want to begin the process of researching. You've already done a lot of groundwork for the research through your reading. However, your next job is to decide which parts of the information you've learned should be included in your reports.

"As a researcher digs in, he develops questions to be answered. I have already chosen three questions I want each of you to answer about your mammal. I've decided on those questions based on the learning we've done in science. I want you to be able to compare certain aspects of the mammals' lives. However, I am also going to let you choose two more questions you want to answer.

"Today's mini-lesson is going to be a little longer than usual. There are two components of this mini-lesson. Usually, I would break them into two lessons (teachers may decide to do this as two lessons depending on the level of their students), but I am going to do them together.

"One of the things I've noticed about the informational texts I like to read is that, while the authors tell me many important things to know, they also include interesting information. My idea is that interesting things really keep me reading. I mean, I think it is all interesting, if I want to know about elephants. But sometimes, I hear a fact that just intrigues me. We've read some books like that this year. Do you remember *Fireflies in the Night* by Judy Hawes? The author told about a boy gathering fireflies with his grandpa. At the same time, I learned a lot of important information about fireflies in the same book.

"I want you all to work hard at including both interesting and important information in your reports. You will make your best decision about the interesting things. I will help you with the important things.

"Now, the other item I want us to deal with is deciding on questions. Here are the three things I've already decided we'll all answer."

Questions to Be Answered

1. Where does your mammal live? (location)

2. What does your mammal eat?

3. Who are your mammal's predators?

"There are other important things you could tell me about your mammals. Can you think of some?

Let's make a list of other ideas. Again, you will have to answer these three questions, and then you will write two more questions to be answered. At least one of those will help you report your interesting information. What are some more important ideas to consider?"

More Ideas for Important Questions

1. What does your mammal look like?

2. What does your mammal use for shelter?

3. Is your mammal a hunter?

"Great, now you have the three required questions and some ideas for other things you might like to find out. What will you do to make sure you include your interesting facts as well? Okay, one of your questions might be 'What is something interesting about your mammal?' That would work.

"Maybe, if you already know the interesting facts you want to include, you could ask a question you know will be answered by the information you want to share. For example, I think there are many interesting things to tell you about an elephant's teeth. I might choose to write the question, 'What is different about an elephant's teeth?'

"Now, do you see why I had you do the reading first? If I didn't already know the things about an elephant's teeth, I wouldn't know to write that question. I really think that you are better researchers when you have a lot of knowledge about your subject.

"Today, I want all of you to decide on the two additional questions you will be asking and answering about your topics. I will be walking around to see them. If I need clarification, I will ask."

Mini-Lesson Focus: Taking Notes

Day 4

It will be your job to model researching for your students and to involve them in some of your research to provide guided practice. Today's lesson will deal with the task of taking notes. It is a difficult concept, and most of us, as adults, have our own methods. Share a method or two with your students. Discerning what is important will be a difficult task for many students, compounded by the decision of what to write down. Model, model, model!

The teacher says:

"One thing I have noticed is that if I ask you all to take notes, you usually write too much. The idea of taking notes is to get just enough down to remind yourselves later. A note will be a few words or a phrase to help you remember what you learned. After taking notes, you will begin writing your reports. I want to spend some time today showing you several different methods and forms for taking notes. The notes only have to make sense to you, and if they don't make sense to you, the work you're doing right now will be wasted time.

"We are going to look at three different ways to record your notes. We've already decided on questions. Now, we have to decide where to write the questions and where to record the answers we find. One of my favorites is a matrix. (If you've already done a biography, your students will be familiar with this.) I will put an example up for you to see.

"So far, the only resources you've become familiar with are the resources you found in the library. Most research does involve reading, but there are other methods for learning information. For example, when our family was at the zoo this summer, we learned a lot about elephants from a man who was volunteering his time and knowledge to any willing listeners. He showed us a cast of an elephant's tooth and knew so much about elephants. It was really hot that day, but we were still willing to stop and listen. My youngest son loves elephants, and we tend to spend extra time near the elephants anyway.

"Some of you might be able to interview a veterinarian about your animals, depending on the types of animals you've chosen. There are also lots of nature shows and videos. You might choose to watch one of the shows and take notes from what you've seen.

"The hard part now, is deciding what to write down and how to write it. Several days from now, you have to be able to look at the things you've written down and still know what they mean. This is one time I am going to tell you to avoid writing complete sentences. A whole sentence takes too much space, and we don't want to copy every word from the resources we've read. Let me show you what I mean."

On the following page is a matrix with limited information about elephants. Use it, or develop one of your own dealing with the topic of research you are using. Walk the students through the process of finding answers to the questions and taking notes to remember the information gathered. It may be necessary to do this mini-lesson over two days. On the first day, work for a while, then let students do some research themselves. Spend the writing time that day circulating to see how well students understand taking notes. If more instruction is needed, use a second day to model solving the exact problems your students are having.

Questions / Resources	What do elephants eat?	Where do elephants live?	What predators does an elephant have?	What is different about an elephant's teeth?
Elephants by Wexo	mostly grass; tree bark and fruit	used to be all over Africa, now in national parks	people! too big for other animals to hunt	6 sets; chewing their food wears them out
Enchanted Learning.com				
St. Louis Zoo volunteer	at the zoo they eat hay, LOTS of it			held one; they weigh 8 pounds each
Encyclopedia				

To model for students the process of taking notes, read excerpts from the resources you've read. Read a whole paragraph or several sentences explaining what elephants eat (or what your chosen mammal eats). Then model, deciding what little bits of information to write down. The difficult part is narrowing sentences to three- or four-word phrases. Again, take two days to do this if the process seems to be difficult for your students. If using a matrix, the paper can be a regular sheet (8½" x 11"). Some teachers have noticed that limiting the size of the boxes can help the students limit the information they include.

If you have decided to use note cards or another method for taking notes, use your mini-lessons to model taking notes in the same format. Again, encourage students to write short phrases rather than complete sentences.

Mini-Lesson Focus: Formatting the Text

Day 5

When young students do research for the first time, or even the first several times, the real emphasis of instruction is on how to do the research. It is a complicated, time-consuming process. For that reason, consider selecting a format for the presentation of the information. There are several books to consider. This mini-lesson will be your chance to model the format your students will use or formats they are able to choose from. If you teach third grade, a common time to introduce research, consider using the information your students find to write a class book. Each student would be responsible for one page.

Three pattern/format ideas to consider:

1. *The Important Book* by Margaret Wise Brown (HarperCollins, 1949)
2. *A is for America: An American Alphabet* by Devin Scillian (Sleeping Bear Press, 2001)

   S is for Show Me: A Missouri Alphabet by Judy Young (Sleeping Bear Press, 2001)

   Any of the Sleeping Bear Press state alphabet books will work.
3. A class big book, alphabet or other

The teacher says:

"I know you all are still gathering information from your resources. It takes a while to take all of your notes. Today, I want to talk to you about what we will do with the information once we have it. There are some books we have read this year that we may use as patterns for writing about our animals. The type of writing we are going to do is called expository writing, and it can be difficult—it can also be dry and boring. Instead, I thought we might borrow some ideas from the authors we've read this year.

"For example, how many of you remember *The Important Book*? The pattern in the book is easy to follow and would allow you to tell all kinds of things about your animals. I was thinking about how I might write about elephants using that pattern. I know I have to be sure to include the information for the three required questions and the two other questions I chose. Let me show you a couple of my pages I am working on."

> The important thing in an African elephant's diet is grass. It also eats tree bark and some kinds of fruit. In zoos, an elephant usually eats hay. It eats twice as much as it needs because it doesn't digest food very well. But, the important thing in an African elephant's diet is grass.

"Do you see how I included other information? I let you know some things I learned about what elephants eat, and the pattern of the book made it easy to decide how to write the sentences. Let me show you one more page about the elephant's teeth."

> The important thing about an elephant's teeth is that it has six different sets. The teeth weigh eight pounds each. They only have four teeth in their mouths. The teeth wear out because the food they chew is so coarse. But, the important thing about an elephant's teeth is that it has six sets.

"I left room at the top for a diagram or illustration to go along with my text. I think *The Important Book* would be an easy format to use and would make writing about your topics a whole lot easier.

"Now, you might also remember us reading *A is for America: An American Alphabet* (Devin Scillian, Sleeping Bear Press, 2001) or *S is for Show Me: A Missouri Alphabet* (Judy Young, Sleeping Bear Press, 2001). These alphabet books also gave me an idea for our research. It takes a long time to write an alphabet book since you each need a special word for each letter. You could probably each get a few letters on one page if they are a little harder to come up with. But, I think you could use this idea for your mammals, too. Now, in the state alphabet books, the verse for each letter rhymes, and I don't want you to think you have to make yours rhyme. We've talked before about how hard it is to rhyme. But, you can write quick explanations of the information and words for the letters, then tell more information in the margins, if you'd like. I tried this out, too. Let me show you what I've done."

A is for Africa,
the country you will find
is home to many elephants,
the big ear kind.

African elephants have large ears, much the same shape as the continent of Africa. They need these large ears to help them stay cool in the heat of the day.

B is for big,
the size of an elephant.
It is the largest animal
on land.

The male African elephant is usually around 10 feet tall and can weigh up to 12,000 pounds.

"You see that I did rhyme one page because it seemed easy to rhyme. I didn't try on the other one, and you can choose the way you would like to do it. The hardest part about the alphabet book will be knowing enough about each animal to come up with one word for all 26 letters!"

(For younger students, third grade or so, you might decide to make one alphabet book for the whole class. If your topic is animals, you might choose animals for each letter, and students could decide which ones to research. Or, an even better option for choice is allowing each student to choose the animal she wants, then let her choose a letter to represent her animal either by name or by one of its features. For example, if you didn't have a student who chose an animal for the letter **Q**, someone might do a rabbit on that page because it is so "quiet." One alphabet book would allow your students to focus on the research and not get tangled up in the writing. This allows next year's teachers to have smoother starts to the research and do more with the writing.)

"If you decide to make an alphabet book, your best first step is to make lists of each word you will use to write about your animals. That will make the writing go much faster. Here is part of my elephant list."

A - Africa	N - nurturing
B - big	O - old
C - calves (what the babies are called)	P -
D - digest	Q - quiet
E - endangered	R -
F - finger (on the trunk)	S - swimmers
G - grass	T - trunk
H - herd	U -
I - ivory	V -
J - jungle	W - wrinkles
K -	X -
L -	Y -
M - mammoth	Z - zoo

"You can see that I still have some gaps. Some letters will be more difficult than others. I may end up using the missing letters to describe something about the elephant. For example, I might use **U** for upper lip. An elephant's trunk is a combination of the upper lip and the nose, and I could talk about that on the **U** page. I will let you choose between these two formats for your information. Right now, you need to continue taking notes from your resources. Tomorrow, we'll talk about organizing your information."

The one format that is not mentioned is a class big book. You might have each child create one large page (half of a sheet of poster board). On that sheet, each student would write approximately as many paragraphs as he had questions. In other words, he would write approximately one paragraph to answer each question. The student might include a map of where the animal lives and any other graphics you want to require. In addition, to make the book more attractive, you might have each student create a border around the page that somehow relates to the animal or theme of the information. With this format, your students will be sticking to the questions they answered. In the other two formats, you can see where they could also pull from any other information they read.

A border to accompany the elephant information might be small elephant heads all around the page, or alternating whole elephants with elephant heads. The hardest part of this project would be modeling how to write those paragraphs. If your students need more practice with writing expository and using topic sentences, this might be an option you'd like to try.

To assemble your big books, place the half pieces of poster board side by side. Use clear packing tape to attach them.

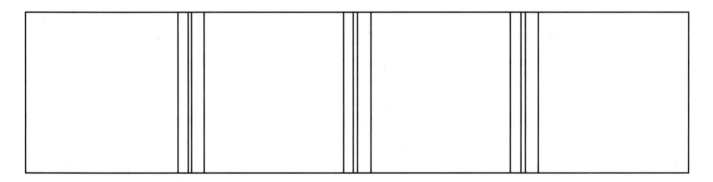

You will fold the pages like an accordion. This allows you to turn the pages of the book as a book or set the entire book up as a display. Do not put any pages on the back of another page. They will all be one-sided and attached with the tape.

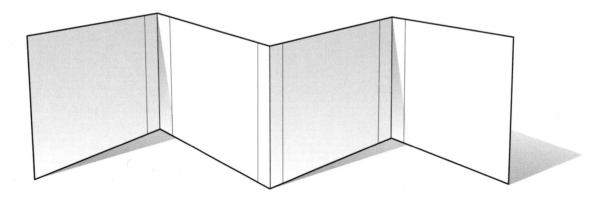

Mini-Lesson Focus: Organizing the Information

Day 6

Once you've decided on the format your students' pieces will take, you will then need to talk about how to organize the information. In the ABC books, the organization is decided by the words chosen for each letter. However, in *The Important Book* format, your students will have to decide which important information they want to mention first. If you are doing a class big book, again they will need to decide how the information should begin and what order it should appear in. If you have any graphic organizers to help them with the process, use them during the modeling of this mini-lesson.

The teacher says:

"For those of you who will be using *The Important Book* pattern, you will need to make some decisions about how to organize your information. Obviously, the ABC books are organized in alphabetical order, so those books won't need a lot of thought about organization.

"When I think back to my page I wrote for *The Important Book* pattern, I wouldn't want that to be my first page. I was telling about what the elephant eats. I think I might like to have some pages that tell what it looks like first. Then, I would tell where the elephant lives and what it eats. Maybe I should make a list of the order I want to put my ideas in. I know I won't remember if I don't."

Important Book about African Elephants

- how it looks
- where it lives
- what it eats
- its predators
- what is different about its teeth
- other interesting facts

"Your lists don't have to be in the same order as mine, but you do need to give them some thought. Think about what your readers would need to know first or what would make sense."

If you will be making a big book with the whole class, you will need to do a lesson on how to present that information. For example, you might tell students that some people draw a reader in by first telling an interesting fact. The elephant piece might start this way, "People only get two sets of teeth, but an elephant gets six sets! The elephant tooth fairy must be really busy." Then, the piece could continue telling why the elephant gets those extra teeth, etc.

Many students' writing is weak because there is no organization. Model different ways your students can organize.

Mini-Lesson Focus: Paragraphs

Day 7

This mini-lesson will be most important if your students are creating a class big book. The other two formats will help your students see how to write their paragraphs. However, it may be necessary to go over this for the informational text to be included in the margins of the ABC books. Spend time modeling how to turn questions into topic sentences or the beginnings of the paragraphs.

The teacher says:

"Today, I want to talk to you about writing paragraphs. We have had several mini-lessons already this year on paragraph writing. However, in expository text, it is much easier to tell when you should start a new paragraph. Each time you change subjects or topics, you will write a new paragraph. In fact, you will have at least as many paragraphs as you have questions. Your page in our class big book will be written to answer each of those questions, and for most of them, you will begin a new paragraph for each new idea. However, if you gathered a lot of information about one question, you may end up with more than one paragraph to answer that question.

"For my paragraphs, I thought about how I wanted to answer the questions, and with some questions, I just turned them into my first sentences. Then, I wrote more sentences to include all of the other information I had gathered. Let me show you how I got started on my page."

African Elephants

People get two sets of teeth, but an elephant gets six! The tooth fairy must stay really busy. An elephant wears down his teeth when he eats. After the set of teeth wears out, he grows a new set. There are only four teeth in an elephant's mouth, and each one weighs eight pounds. But, after the sixth set wears out, an elephant won't grow any more. Usually, an elephant dies soon after his last set of teeth wears out.

The African elephants mostly eat grass. It makes up almost all of their diet. But, they also eat tree bark and fruit. Elephants have to eat twice as much as they need because they can't digest their food very well. All of that extra chewing really wears out their teeth, and it means that they spend a lot of time eating.

"If you are working on an ABC book, you will write paragraphs that explain the little verse you wrote for each letter. For example, when I said 'A is for Africa,' look at what I wrote on the bottom of that page."

A is for Africa,
the country you will find
is home to many elephants,
the big ear kind.

African elephants have large ears, much the same shape as the continent of Africa. They need these large ears to help them stay cool in the heat of the day.

"In the verse, I said something about the 'big ear kind,' so in my paragraph I had to explain what that means. I could also add a paragraph about where you find elephants in Africa. So, for the ABC books, look at your verses to see how to start your paragraphs."

Spend as much time on writing paragraphs as your students need. The best way to make the writing easier is to provide plenty of time to read prior to the writing. The paragraphs will come easily when most of the knowledge is coming from the readers/writers rather than the writers having to look back at books to find information to include.

Mini-Lesson Focus: Features of Nonfiction Text

Day 8

During this lesson, model for students some of the features found in informational text. It is much easier if the same type of lesson has already been given in reading. Decide what features you might want your students to include. For example, they could create indexes at the backs of the books. Illustrations could include labels or diagrams. Perhaps they could download real photographs to combine with self-made illustrations. Consider what would be most appropriate to accompany the finished product you have decided on. Even *The Important Book* pattern could be illustrated with diagrams and could include captions. If you are making a class big book, you could also include headings. Nonfiction text looks different on a page, and the reader relies on certain clues to know that the text provides facts, not a story.

The teacher says:

"Today, we are going to look at the features you will include to show you are writing expository, or informational text. Remember when we made a list of things that are clues for us as readers? One day we were reading a *Scholastic News*, and we made a list of the features it included. There were things like captions, headings, charts, graphs, maps, labels, and real photographs. Those are features authors use to cue the readers. When we are reading and we see those things, we know we are reading informational text. Well, if that is the case, we need to make sure we include some of those things in our text."

(If you are going to require certain features, use those as the thrust of this mini-lesson. If you will be letting students choose from the features you've mentioned, model the ones you've chosen for your own writing.)

A is for Africa,
the country you will find
is home to many elephants,
the big ear kind.

African elephants have large ears, much the same shape as the continent of Africa. They need these large ears to help them stay cool in the heat of the day.

B is for big,
the size of an elephant.
It is the largest animal
on land.

The male African elephant is usually around 10 feet tall and can weigh up to 12, 000 pounds.

"On this page, for the letter **A**, I know I want to include a drawing of an elephant with a label on his ear. I will write on the label, 'large ears the shape of Africa.' I also want a small map of the African continent in the upper right-hand corner, maybe indicating the areas where elephants are found. On my **B** page, I think I want to draw an elephant and a man to show the comparison of how much bigger an elephant is. So, on these two pages I've used a label, a diagram, a map, and a comparison illustration.

"If I think about my important book, I would also include illustrations and diagrams. Let's look at an example."

The important thing in an African elephant's diet is grass. It also eats tree bark and some kinds of fruit. In zoos, an elephant usually eats hay. It eats twice as much as it needs because it doesn't digest food very well. But, the important thing in an African elephant's diet is grass.

"On this page, I might have something like an illustration showing how much grass an elephant eats in a year. I saw a picture kind of like that in my *Elephants*. I think that helps me realize how much an elephant really eats. I would have to write a caption under the picture or the reader wouldn't know why there was so much grass there."

For these two formats, a table of contents won't be applicable. However, if you write a class big book, it would be a great time to model writing a table of contents. An index could be added to any of these texts, but you would need to decide how much time to devote to that particular feature. It could become rather labor intensive.

Later in the Year—Getting Better!

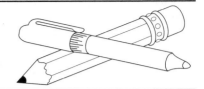

Mini-lessons for later in the year are the "icing on the cake." Students learn how their writing can be a gift to someone they care about, how journals and diaries can help them sharpen their writing or reflect upon their experiences, and how to write traditional tales. There is a set of focused writing lessons on writing traditional tales—a fun genre at the end of the year!

The year ends with a publishing and author celebration in which everyone savors their accomplishments and reflects on how far they have come as writers. Some teachers may not get to all of the end of the year mini-lessons because of testing time. The lessons we have included at the end of the year are some of the easiest and most fun lessons. Upper-grade teachers and students work hard all year long, so it is nice to have some fun after "testing time" at the end of the year. The lessons for later in the year include:

Focused Writing: Traditional Tales (Craft)

>   Day 1: Characteristics of the Pourquoi

>   Day 2: Choosing an Element in Nature

>   Day 3: Sketching Out the Plot

>   Day 4: Setting

>   Day 5: Other Characters in the Story

>   Day 6: Writing the Story

Journals/Diaries (Craft)

Publishing and Celebrating Writing (Procedures)

Focused Writing: Traditional Tales (Craft)

Writing fiction is difficult. It is much easier to write about things you know, places you've been, or experiences you've had. Therefore, when approaching the fiction genres, it is often less threatening to require students to write a fiction genre they are very familiar with and with fewer expectations. Traditional tales come in many forms: fairy tales, tall tales, fables, pourquois, legends, etc. While these types of stories have often been a part of the students' repertoires for a large number of years, it will still be essential to read many examples of the genre prior to asking students to write.

Fiction is difficult because of the many facets that are needed. The predictability of the traditional tale creates a much easier form of fiction to write—characters will not need to be well-developed, plot usually follows a pattern, etc. For the purpose of this book, the traditional tale modeled will be a pourquoi. However, we feel that you could use a similar approach with any of the traditional tales. A supportive resource is *Reading and Writing Literary Genres* by Kathleen Buss and Lee Karnowski (International Reading Association, 2000). It is useful in determining the characteristics of many literary genres.

Prior to the first mini-lesson, make sure that you have read many examples of pourquois (or the genre of your choosing) and have many examples available during the time of writing. Students may want to refer back to these texts for ideas. As you decide which type of traditional tale for students to write, choose one you have the resources to support and one you feel confident in modeling during the mini-lessons.

As with all other focused writing examples, you will be writing a class example as part of the mini-lessons. In fact, prior to doing these lessons, it would be helpful for you to write a traditional tale of your own. When you begin modeling, it will be much easier to think aloud about your writing if you've already had the experience.

Traditional Tales

Day 1:   Characteristics of the Pourquoi

Day 2:   Choosing an Element in Nature

Day 3:   Sketching Out the Plot

Day 4:   Setting

Day 5:   Other Characters in the Story

Day 6:   Writing the Story

Mini-Lesson Focus: Characteristics of the Pourquoi

Day 1

Each type of traditional tale has its own characteristics. For the purpose of the pourquoi, we will discuss them in depth. At the end of the lessons, you will also find a general listing of the characteristics of other traditional tales. Also, remember *Reading and Writing Literary Genres* is a wonderful resource on genre characteristics. If this is the first time your students have written in the traditional tale genre you choose, use this first lesson to teach the characteristics. If it is more familiar to students, ask for input with questions like, "Who remembers some of the unique qualities of a fairy tale?"

The teacher says:

"Today, we are beginning our mini-lessons to teach us how to write a pourquoi of our own. I've read you many pourquois, and some of you have read others on you own. Our purpose today is to make a list of the characteristics of this genre. In other words, what makes it unique? How is it different than other traditional tales or even other fiction?

"Think back about some of the books we've read. If you remember, the word pourquoi is the French word for why. Therefore, these stories tell why something is the way it is in nature. Think about the very titles of books we've read: *Why Mosquitoes Buzz in People's Ears* and *Why the Sun and the Moon Live in the Sky*. The title of the pourquoi tells you exactly what will be explained by the story.

"So, our first characteristic is: something that occurs in nature is explained. If you think about that, you can see why, so often, animals are the main characters. A pourquoi can have people, too, but more often the characters will be animals. The characters don't even have to be well-developed. In a pourquoi, we assume that the reader knows what type of character the person or animal in the story is. For example, the fox is often portrayed as tricky or sly. The mouse scurries, is a hard worker, etc. A lion would command respect or fear from other animals. Yet, you don't have to worry too much about showing these traits—they are just assumed.

"Another element that is addressed is the setting. However, the setting is not that important. The story will take place in a time and place, but again, it is stated at the beginning and not dwelt on. The culture of that setting is again assumed. Choosing a place your readers know well will be helpful.

"In the plot of your story, the whole problem will be centered on the main character. The reason for the story is to explain how things in nature evolved. So, your character's problem will drive the plot, and all of the actions in the story happen to change the character. Many times, the story begins by telling how things used to be. Then, because of the actions in the story, things are the way they are now.

"So, let's list the characteristics we've decided on so far. This list will help you as you begin to decide on your own characters and plot."

Pourquois

1. An element of nature is explained.

2. Main character is flat or not well-developed; traits are assumed.

3. Setting is established, but culture is known to the reader.

4. Plot is focused on the one problem established in the title.

Mini-Lesson Focus: Choosing an Element in Nature

Day 2

As you work with students to list options for their pourquois, remember that it is fine if they "rewrite" the reason something has happened. For example, a student may have a better reason for why mosquitoes buzz in people's ears. If he wants to rewrite his own version, that shouldn't be a problem. Spend today working with students to brainstorm options for how the characters in nature became the way they are. Encourage your students to either pull from this list or come up with their own ideas. The stories, however, must be original.

The teacher says:

"Today, we want to work together to brainstorm a list of possibilities for elements in nature you might describe. During writing time today, you will be spending time deciding on the topics for your own pourquois. It is fine for you to come up with your very own, or to use the list we will brainstorm for ideas or choices. Here are some topics I have thought of."

Pourquoi Topics

1. How an elephant got a long trunk
2. Why a zebra has stripes
3. How the camel got his humps
4. Why geese fly in a V

"Now, these are just some of my ideas. What are some of the ideas you are thinking about?"

The teacher decides how many ideas he wants to list before he sends students off to work on their own topics. They may want to work on more than just ideas or titles. It is fine for them to start, but the teacher reminds them that he hopes to provide some more information for how to write a pourquoi in the next few days.

Also, as the teacher lists a few of his own ideas, he decides to try some more modern phenomena such as, "why the dad rules the remote control" and "why the computer loses certain information." (If you want your class pourquois to resemble the pourquois you have been reading, don't even suggest these things. But, if you like the option of having them modernized, be sure to include some modern suggestions on your list.)

Looking Ahead

In preparation for tomorrow's lesson, you will need to choose one of your example topics or another topic you would like to write on. Decide on the basic plot of the story.

Mini-Lesson Focus: Sketching Out the Plot

Day 3

The plot of this genre is not complex. It is a series of actions used to resolve the one problem established in the title. There is only one problem in the story, and the stereotypical characters go through a series of events to solve that problem. Give your students suggestions for how to develop this simple plot through some prewriting/brainstorming activities. The author needs to know what the problem is and how it is solved before writing.

The teacher says:

"I think for the class pourquoi, I am going to choose the title *Why the Donkey Is Stubborn*. I chose this title because it is a characteristic of donkeys that most people know. As I get ready to write my story, I need to do a lot of thinking about how the donkey used to be and how he is going to end up stubborn.

"I want to sketch my basic story out, so I don't have to spend so much time wondering what is going to happen as I write. I think it will help you if you do the same thing. Today, I will show you a couple of ways to do some brainstorming, and you can choose the method that works best for you.

"I know that to start my story, I need to think about how donkeys used to be. I'll say that donkeys used to be kind and generous and would do anything for anyone. I am going to start with a basic chart that says beginning, middle, and end."

Beginning

Donkeys were loving and kind. They were the best helpers because they would do anything for anyone.

Middle

Lots of animals are going to take advantage of the donkey. Everyone will be asking him to do things for them without being thankful.

End

The donkey is going to get mad, kick up his heels, and refuse to help others again.

"As I fill in this chart, I have my basic plot in place. I know in my head, and on paper now, that the donkey is going to change from being kind and generous to being stubborn and hard-headed. I even have an idea for how that is going to happen. However, I think it might help me even more if I add some details to my beginning, middle, and end. I wrote that lots of animals would ask for help, who will those animals be? What will they ask for? I want to make a list, so it will be easier to write the story."

Writing Mini-Lessons for Upper Grades: The Big-Blocks™ Approach

Describe how gentle donkeys were.

Dog - needed help reaching a limb

Squirrel - needed a boost to the tree

Chicken - wanted protection from Fox

Donkey will feel unappreciated.

"Now, as you look at the elements you chose yesterday, think about a brainstorming strategy for making some decisions about your plot. You could use a Beginning-Middle-End box if you think that would help. Or, try a web for your story. Even a list would be a good way to think about the order in which things will happen and who will be included."

Looking Ahead

In preparation for tomorrow's lesson, decide where your story should take place and how the culture will affect the characters.

Mini-Lesson Focus: Setting

Day 4

As was mentioned in the Day 1 mini-lesson (page 140), the setting needs to be established in the beginning of the story, but much about the setting is assumed. The setting should fit the characters and the problem and include the time in history in which the story took place. The setting creates the backdrop for solving this problem in nature. Today's mini-lesson won't be long. You will model for students the ways to choose a setting and make it an integral part of their stories.

The teacher says:

"Today, I need to decide where my story about my donkey will take place. I remember when we read the story of *Why the Sun and the Moon Live in the Sky*, the story was from long ago, and most of it took place in that hut. In fact, most pourquois take place long ago. Some are set way back in history, but others are more recent.

"As I thought about my story with the donkey, I decided that a farm would be a good setting. Donkeys have been a part of farms for a long time. I think my farm will be from long ago, you know, before cars and electricity. Back then, horses and donkeys played a very important part on the farm. They helped the farmer work by plowing and hauling. They could also provide transportation by pulling wagons or carrying riders.

"So, as I map out my story today, it looks like this."

Title: Why the Donkey Is So Stubborn

Setting: a farm, long ago

Characters: donkey, dog, chicken, squirrel, farmer

Problem: Donkey feels unappreciated because he has been very helpful to the other animals, and no one helps him. He begins to get frustrated.

Solution: Donkey becomes very unfriendly and stubborn, therefore, no one asks for his help anymore.

"As you begin to work on your stories today, you may continue working on the sketch of your plot, and you will also need to consider your setting. Where would it make sense for your story to take place? What time period in history would work for this story? Also, think about how you will establish the setting from the beginning."

Looking Ahead

In tomorrow's lesson you will begin a discussion of the other characters in your pourquoi. What stereotypical characteristics do they portray?

Mini-Lesson Focus: Other Characters in the Story

Day 5

For the story you are writing, you will want to choose some characters who can display stereotypical traits. Pourquois work on the assumption that the reader knows the character for who or what she really is.

The teacher says:

"When I listed my beginning, middle, and end, I told you some of the other characters I would be including in my pourquoi. Today, I want to really think about those characters and what type of 'person' I expect them to be. Remember that in a pourquoi, we exaggerate or emphasize the things we know about certain animals or people.

"For example, I have a dog as one of my other characters, and I think I will emphasize his knowing that he is supposed to be 'man's best friend.' Maybe he will even think he is a little better than the donkey because he is the 'farmer's best friend.' Then, I also have a squirrel. What do we know about squirrels? I guess I always think of them as being very busy, preparing for the winter days ahead, etc. I'll try to include that somehow, too. Then, my last character is a chicken. Hmmm . . . chickens are just kind of silly. I mean they are birds, but they can't really fly. I also know they are afraid of foxes. I think I will use that in my part about the chicken.

"See, it is important to think about the other characters who will be a part of the action in your stories. They will be a big part of why your characters make the changes they make.

"As you continue working today, think about those other characters and how you can use the things people already know about them to help you."

Looking Ahead

For tomorrow, you will want to have a portion of your pourquoi written to share with the class. In fact, as mentioned in the introduction, this whole series of mini-lessons will be easier to teach if you've already gone through the steps. Then, you will also have things to share during mini-lesson time. You may have to create it all again as if it is the first time, but your instruction will come more easily if you have been through the process.

Mini-Lesson Focus: Writing the Story

Day 6

It is time to share aloud the thinking you do as you write in front of the students. It is fine if you bring in the piece that you have already begun. You can add to it in front of the students. Either do all or some of the writing in front of them today; refer back to your plot sketches and the details you know you want to include. Students need to see you write, hear that you have the same frustrations, and see the importance of reading and rereading what has been written. As Nancie Atwell says, take off the top of your head while you teach (1998).

The teacher says:

"I have finally begun writing my pourquoi. I started my story last night, so that I could share part of it with you today. I want to keep adding to it, and I will also do some of the adding-on during our mini-lesson. Let me show you what I have so far."

Why the Donkey Is So Stubborn

Back during the days of candlelight and cooking over a fire, Donkey was an important part of the farming family. Donkey knew how much the farmer depended on him for all of the hard work he needed to do. Donkey was a gentle and loving animal. He was always happy to help out the farmer with his chores.

Other animals knew how helpful Donkey could be, as well. They often depended on him to help them, too.

"I started my story this way, and I want to reread what I have so far and then begin to add on. Every time you stop and start again, you will want to read what you have written so far and decide if it says exactly what you want it to say. I am still not sure that I like my lead. I am trying to let the reader know that it takes place before electricity, but I am not sure that the words I chose are the best choices."

The teacher continues in this manner, adding to the story in front of the class and thinking aloud about the decisions he makes as the author.

Other Ideas Connected to Writing a Traditional Tale

Choose an audience to write the stories for (perhaps a younger grade level might be interested in hearing the stories)

After revision and editing, do a mini-lesson on illustrating the stories

Other Genre Characteristics

Fable

- begins with the moral
- most characters are animals
- story is very brief
- plot is, again, connected to one problem
- characters are stereotypical, again

Fairy Tale

- good vs. evil
- make-believe
- some use elements of magic

Fractured Fairy Tale

- begins with a well-known fairy tale
- alters the course of action
- sometimes eaiser to begin with the end in mind

Mini-Lesson Focus: Diary and Journal Writing (Craft)

All kinds of people keep journals and diaries. People record the everyday events of their lives and the events and issues that concern them. These are personal records; they are not intended for publication. Some journals of famous people have survived for years and give us a glimpse of what life was like for Anne Frank hiding from the Nazis, or Lewis and Clark traveling across the country.

During the year, you've been writing daily with your students. As you prepare to send them home for the summer, encourage them to continue their daily writing. The personal writing genres are not really addressed in Writer's Workshop because in Writer's Workshop, we write to be read. However, just before the end of the year, it is a good time to talk about keeping dairies and journals with your students.

The teacher says:

"This year I have been so impressed with your hard work as writers. You've written every day, and you've learned so much about writing. I know you can look back at some of the pieces you wrote at the beginning of the year, and you can see the difference. I am really proud of you.

"As you get ready for summer, I am really hopeful that you will continue your journeys as authors and writers. I think that you have realized this year that writing gets easier the more you write. I don't want you to go for three months without writing—it is just too important. Now, I am not giving you home-work for the summer, but I do want to talk to you about some options for writing during vacation.

"This year, you all have written to be read by an audience. You've chosen to publish pieces to share with your peers, your parents, and other visitors. This summer, you might want to spend some time writing in a genre that is really written only for you. I am sure you are all familiar with diaries and journals. We laugh about stories of little brothers stealing their sisters' diaries and reading all that has been written.

"But seriously, a diary or journal can be a great way to record events, feelings, fears, and stories in your life. It is possible that after keeping that journal this summer, you find that it is full of writing ideas for next year.

"Later in your life, you will truly enjoy going back to journals and reading what you've written. It will make you laugh, as you wonder how something so small could have been so important. It might even make you cry, as you realize something that hurt in the past still hurts.

"So, today's mini-lesson is just an encouragement to keep on writing. Put your thoughts on paper and cherish the time you spend writing them. As I write today, I will not talk aloud. I will write, and you can read what I have to say."

I hope that you spend the summer reading and writing. I hope that you find some wonderful new authors who become your friends and you want to spend some time each day with them. I hope that you find time to write about what is important in your lives and share your inner thoughts and feelings with yourselves. It helps you know who you are and what you like when you put your thoughts on paper.

Other Ideas for Diary and Journal Writing

Sharing Diaries and Journals from Your Past

If you choose to, you could bring in examples of a diary and a journal. You might even read excerpts of a journal you've kept yourself and one from a family member that you now possess.

Sharing Diaries and Journals from Your Students

If you have a student who is willing, share an example of his journal writing about a trip or person.

Sharing the Different Types of Journals or Diaries

There are journals and diaries to keep all through the school year if desired.

Talk about the different kinds of journals and model typical writing for each.

Personal Journals
Students write about events in their own lives and other topics of special interest in personal journals. These journals are the most private type.

Today, I came to school early. I wanted to get my desk cleaned off before the holidays. So, I . . . .

Dialogue Journals
Dialogue journals are similar to personal journals except that the entries are written to be shared with the teacher or a classmate. The person who receives the journal reads the entry and responds to it. These journals are like written conversations.

Dear Jennifer,

How did you remember it was my birthday? We went to Cities Café to eat, and then went shopping at the mall. I got a new sweater. It was just what I had been looking for.

Karen

Dear Karen,

I remembered your birthday because it is a few days before my mother's birthday. I was wondering what you did. I can't wait to see your new sweater. When do you think you will wear it?

Jennifer

Reading Logs
In reading logs, students respond to stories, poems, or selections they are reading in school or at home. The students may write, draw, and make diagrams or charts to respond to their reading.

While I was reading Harry Potter, I could imagine his aunt, uncle, and cousin. I believe I know some people that act just like them. I felt sorry for Harry sleeping in that small hall closet. He . . . .

Learning Logs
Students write in learning logs as a part of social studies, science, or math. They do quick writes about what they are learning. They talk about the things they understand and don't understand.

In math today, we were doing long division, and I finally understood just what to do.

Mini-Lesson Focus: Publishing and Celebrating Writing (Procedures)

The focus of a good writing program is students as authors. Setting aside time for your students to share their writing is part of the writing process. It also gives students opportunities to develop listening and speaking skills, which are part of an elementary language arts program. Most days, after writing, students get to share something they have written in an Author's Chair format (page 21).

Publishing some of this writing is an important part of writing. When publishing occurs in classrooms, students have a reason to revise ("make it better") and edit ("make it right"). We can let our students have an even wider audience by having a Young Authors' Conference and inviting family and friends or another class. If your students have been publishing for most of the year, then they just choose one book each, and maybe make nicer coves, fix typos, draw nicer illustrations, etc. Without much work, you are ready to celebrate their writing.

If you have not been publishing, but your students have been writing in notebooks or folders, or if you have been saving some writing on computer discs, then you already have the pieces that will become your books.

The teacher tells students about the upcoming Young Authors' Celebration and about the books they will share with family and friends. Then, he shows them how they will choose their books and get ready.

The teacher thinks aloud about her writing:

"These are some books (pieces) I have written this year. Let me read them to you, and you help me decide which one is best or which you think other people might like."

The teacher reads two or three of his stories or pieces he has taken to final copy. Since he has not been publishing all year like the students in his class, he does not have as many books as his students, so he has to use final drafts and explains this to them.

The teacher talks about each piece—what she liked and what she thinks other people might like about it:

"I think people might like my tale, *Why the Donkey Is So Stubborn*. It seems that everyone likes a story with a twist to it. Some people may want to read my biography to find out what I wrote about Martin Luther King, Jr. I also have lots of good stories about my family—sometimes I like those more than other people do because they have so many memories. But, I am going to choose the story I just finished, *Why the Donkey Is So Stubborn*, to make into my book for our Young Authors' Conference."

Next, the teacher goes through the publishing steps on pages 62 and 63:

He chooses a book to put his writing in (many teachers have parents help bind enough books for all the students in their classes to use for the Young Authors' Celebrations). Each student chooses a blank book and writes her final copy inside. (They could also type their final drafts on the computer, print them, and cut the text to fit the pages. Other teachers have parents bind the books after the students finish writing and illustrating them. Some teachers let older students do books in the shapes of their stories or informational pieces. No matter how you do it, for each book you will need: a back and front cover, a title page, a dedication to be placed on the back of the title page, approximately eight pages for the student's writing, and an About the Author page.)

Other Ideas for Publishing and Celebrating Writing

Writing an Invitation with the Class for the Young Authors' Celebration or Tea

Tell students about the invitations they need to send to their families and friends. Create one together. Let them copy and illustrate the invitations they need.

> You are invited to our Young Authors' Celebration (or Tea).
>
> Who: Family and Friends
>
> When: May 12, 2003 at 1:00 P.M.
>
> Where: Room 4, Montgomery City Elementary
>
> We hope you can come celebrate our writing with us!

Publishing a Class Magazine

A collection of individual pieces that are typed, copied, and collated. These class magazines can be themed (friends, holiday, our state, our country, etc.) or contain a specific genre.

Publishing a School Magazine

This format features all kinds of writing from students at all grade levels and is published a certain number of times a year, or once at the end of the year!

Publishing a Year Book

Put together a book about the year's events and happenings. This is a memory of the year containing stories and articles written by the students.

Getting Students' Work in Local Newspapers

Local newspapers are often glad to carry students' work at special times throughout the year. Many papers feature a column about school happenings and students' writing.

Helping Students Enter Writing Contests

Many schools and school districts have writing contests. Students are usually given a theme to write about. There are also state and national contests run by different organizations. If you have students who like to write and who write well, be on the lookout for ways for them to win!

Reading Students' Work on the Intercom

Songs, poems, stories, and informational pieces written by the students can be shared either by the students themselves, or the principal, over the intercom. This is another way for students' work to be recognized.

Creating a Class Bulletin Board

Create a bulletin board where students can go public with their writing. After they go through the writing process, students copy over their finished pieces in their best handwriting or type them on the computer. Then, they "make it public" for all to see on the bulletin board titled "Our Best Writing," "Awesome Authors," etc.

Sharing with Other Classrooms (same grade level or a different one)

Classes can write letters to each other, and they can set aside a special time to share their writing, too. Some classes do this activity each month, once a semester, or once a year.

References

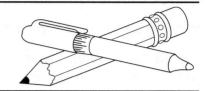

Professional References

Atwell, Nancie (1998) *In the Middle: New Understandings About Writing, Reading and Learning.* Portsmouth, NH: Heinemann.

Atwell, Nancie (2002) *Lessons That Change Writers.* Portsmouth, NH: Heinemann.

Buss, Kathleen and Karnowski, Lee (2000) *Reading and Writing Literary Genres.* Newark, DE: International Reading Association

Calkins, Lucy (1994) *The Art of Teaching Writing.* Portsmouth, NH: Heinemann.

Fletcher, Ralph and Portalupi, JoAnn (1998) *Craft Lessons: Teaching Writing K-8.* Portland, ME: Stenhouse Publishers.

Rief, Linda (1992) *Seeking Diversity: Language Arts with Adolescents.* Portsmouth, NH: Heinemann.

Robb, Laura (2000) *Teaching Reading in Middle School.* New York, NY: Scholastic.

References

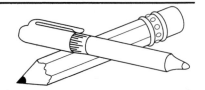

Children's Books Cited

A is for America: An American Alphabet Devin Scillian (Sleeping Bear Press, 2001).

Abe Lincoln's Hat by Martha Brenner (Scholastic, 1994).

And Then What Happened, Paul Revere? Jean Fritz (Putnam & Grosset Group, 1973).

Anne of Green Gables by Lucy Maud Montgomery (Putnam, 1908, Reprint, 1983).

Bloomers! by Rhoda Blumberg (Aladdin, 1993).

Bridge to Terabithia by Katherine Paterson (HarperTrophy, 1987).

Bully for You, Teddy Roosevelt! by Jean Fritz (Putnam & Grosset Group, 1991).

Can't You Make Them Behave, King George? by Jean Fritz (Coward-McCann, 1976).

Captain Underpants by Dav Pilkey (Scholastic, 1997).

Charlotte's Web by E. B. White (HarperTrophy, 1999).

The Cricket in Times Square by George Shelden (Dell Publishing Co., 1975).

Duke Ellington: The Piano Prince and His Orchestra by Andrea Davis Pinkney (Disney Press, 1998).

Elephants by John Bonnett Wexo (Wildlife Education, LTD., 1994).

Fireflies in the Night by Judy Hawes (Scott Foresman, 1991).

Freedom Train: The Story of Harriet Tubman by Dorothy Sterling (Scholastic, 1991).

Georgia O'Keeffe by by Mike Venezia (Children's Press, 1993).

Harriet Tubman: The Road to Freedom by Rae Bains (Troll Communications, 1990).

Harry Potter and the Chamber of Secrets by J. K. Rowling (Scholastic, 1999).

References

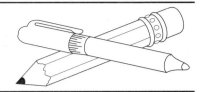

Harry Potter and the Goblet of Fire by J. K. Rowling (Scholastic, 2000).

Harry Potter and the Prisoner of Azkaban by J. K. Rowling (Scholastic, 2000).

Harry Potter and the Sorcerer's Stone by J. K. Rowling (Scholastic, 1998).

How I Spent My Summer Vacation by Mark Teague (Crown Publishing, Inc., 1996).

I Have a Dream: The Story of Martin Luther King by Margaret Davidson (Scholastic, 1994).

The Important Book by Margaret Wise Brown (HarperCollins, 1949).

John Henry by Julius Lester (Penguin, 1999).

Lou Gehrig: The Luckiest Man by David Adler (Harcourt Brace, 1997).

Maniac Magee by Jerry Spinelli (Little Brown & Co, 1990). (Scholastic, 1991).

Maya Angelou Journey of the Heart by Jayne Pettit (Puffin Books, 1996).

Meet Maya Angelou by V. Spain (Random House, 1994).

My Great Aunt Arizona by Gloria Houston (HarperCollins, 1992).

Number the Stars by Lois Lowry (Houghton Mifflin Co., 1989).

A Picture Book of Abraham Lincoln by David Adler (Holiday House, 1990).

A Picture Book of Benjamin Franklin by David Adler (Holiday House, 1990).

A Picture Book of Harriet Tubman by David Adler (Holiday House, 1992).

A Picture Book of Martin Luther King, Jr. by David Adler (Scholastic, 1989).

Ramona Quimby, Age 8 by Beverly Cleary (William Morrow/Avon, 1981).

S is for Show Me: A Missouri Alphabet by Judy Young (Sleeping Bear Press, 2001).

References

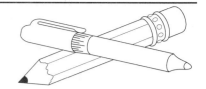

The Secret of NIMH by Robert C. O'Brien (Scholastic, 1982).

Snowshoe Thompson by Nancy Levinson (HarperCollins, 1992).

The Story of Harriet Tubman: Conductor of the Underground Railroad by Kate McMullan (Bantam Doubleday Dell, 1991).

Teammates by Peter Golenbock (Harcourt Brace, 1990).

The True Story of the Three Pigs by Jon Scieszka (Viking Penguin, 1989).

Tuck Everlasting by Natalie Babbit (Farrar, Straus, & Giroux, 1975).

The Velveteen Rabbit by Margery Williams (Western Publishing Company, 1990).

What's the Big Idea, Ben Franklin? by Jean Fritz (Putnam & Grosset Group, 1976).

When I Was Little: A Four-Year-Old's Memory of Her Youth by Jamie Lee Curtis (HarperCollins, 1993).

When I Was Young In the Mountains by Cynthia Rylant (E. P. Dutton, 1993).

Why Mosquitoes Buzz in People's Ears by Vera Aardema (Dial, 1975).

Why the Sun and the Moon Live in the Sky by E. Dayrell (Houghton Mifflin, 1990).

Wilma Unlimited: How Wilma Rudolph Became the World's Fastest Woman by Kathleen Krull (Harcourt Brace, 1996).

Wombat Divine by Mem Fox (Harcourt Brace, 1995).

Other Books Cited

The Rainmaker by John Grisham (Island Books, 1996)

References

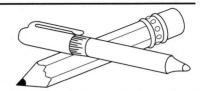

Children's Magazines Cited

National Geographic World

Students Discover

Voices in the Middle

Weekly Reader

Zoo Books

Other Magazines Cited

Newsweek

People

Time

Matrix Template

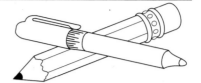

Questions / Resources							

Story Pattern

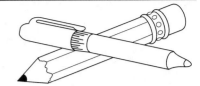

wanted to:

so:

This character:

but:

Writing Mini-Lessons for the Upper Grades: The Big-Blocks™ Approach

Proofreader's Marks

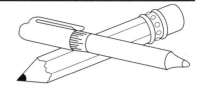

∧	Add, insert
ℐ	Delete, take away
≡	Capitalize
/	Make lowercase
∿	Reverse order of letters
⊙	Add a period
∧	Add (insert) a comma
∨	Add an apostrophe
🔵sp	Check spelling

Notes

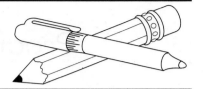